To
Carol and Robbie

With Love from
Marilyn and Drew

Phil. 1:3-11

NORTH LEITH PARISH CHURCH
The First 500 Years

NORTH LEITH PARISH CHURCH
The First 500 Years

Dr James S Marshall

SAINT ANDREW PRESS

EDINBURGH

First published in 1993
by Saint Andrew Press
on behalf of
North Leith Parish Church

Copyright © North Leith Parish Church 1992

ISBN 0–86153–160–4 (Paper)
ISBN 0–86153–161–2 (Cased)

British Library Cataloguing in Publication Data
A catalogue record for this book is available from the British Library.

ISBN 0–86153–160–4 (Paper)
ISBN 0–86153–161–2 (Cased)

Typeset by J&L Composition Ltd, Filey, North Yorkshire
Printed and bound by Athenaeum Press Ltd, Newcastle upon Tyne

Contents

Preface

When the planning began for the 500th Anniversary of a Christian presence in North Leith, it became obvious early on that it would be important to include a history of the Parish throughout the period. No complete history existed. A useful booklet had been produced for an earlier Anniversary but it never purported to be a definitive history. It was also obvious that to do justice to the subject we would require as author someone who was well acquainted with the history of the area and had a love for it. Dr James Marshall had written *The Life and Times of Leith*, which had been published in 1986, and is a history of Leith as a whole. His breadth of knowledge and scholarship and his deep affection for Leith were well known. So it was with great relief and much gratitude that we learnt of his willingness to undertake the writing of this history. And we were not disappointed. The result of nearly two years work and of a lifetime steeped in his subject is now here for us all to share and enjoy. We are all deeply indebted to him for undertaking this task and especially for having set the life and history of the Church so clearly in the context of all that was happening in Leith and the wider world at the time.

It is only when the Church has lost its way that it has become detached from the community which it serves and the life around it. This history makes clear that this has rarely happened over the five hundred years in North Leith. During these years the Church, however stumblingly, has tried to remain true to her Master's calling to be both salt and light to those around. I pray that the same may be true in the next five hundred years.

For every infantryman in any Army, there are supposed to be at least ten working behind the lines to support them. So here, behind Dr Marshall, there have been others to whom I would like to express great gratitude. Our Church History group comprised Miss Anne Murray and Mrs Betty Mackenzie together with our Archivist Dr Barbara Horn of Register House, who all contributed so much by their research and personal insights. The photographs, which add so much to the history, were contributed by the joint efforts of two elders—one from North Leith, the other from South Leith—Norman Lindsay and Joyce Matthews and I am most grateful for their thorough and painstaking work in ensuring the highest standard.

Finally I would like to thank our kirk session for their vision and enthusiasm in 'sponsoring' this project and last but not least our publishers, St Andrew Press, for their helpful assistance from the first interview to the first printed copy.

May this history and the efforts of them all be a source of inspiration to all of you who read this; as we take our first steps towards the next five hundred.

Alistair McGregor
Minister

Foreword

Five centuries of divine worship and community involvement, caring for the poor and the sick, offering moral and spiritual leadership—five hundred years of striving to promote Christ's kingdom in the hearts and lives of the population is surely reason enough to tell the story of it all. Of course there were failures and mistakes, as well as far-seeing decisions and actions through these generations, but it has been a privilege to discover and weave together the strands of the tapestry recording the pilgrimage of the congregation of North Leith. The small company who worshipped in St Ninian's Chapel in the closing years of the fifteenth century can have had no conception of the world of the late twentieth century, or of their descendants, a numerous congregation aspiring to the same ends and serving the same Master.

I have been guided and encouraged in this work by Miss Anne Murray, grand-daughter of the Rev Dr William Smith, the nationally known minister of North Leith in mid-Victorian times, by Mrs Betty Mackenzie, wife of a former session clerk, knowledgeable on the old Bonnington congregation, and especially by Dr Barbara Horn of the Scottish Record Office, who willingly and painstakingly read through the early kirk session minutes and heritors' records. Mr Norman Lindsay has attended to the illustrations, and from first to last my good friend Alistair McGregor, present minister of North Leith, has with his enthusiasm kept the project going and finally has seen the book through the press.

J S M

CHAPTER 1

The Birth of the Parish

When King David I set up the Abbey of the Holy Rood in the twelfth century he endowed it with extensive lands. These acres included the area bounded by the Water of Leith which later became North Leith. The river then separated the land of Holy Rood from the estates of the de Lestalrics. This was all open country, gently shelving towards the sea. Leith then consisted of a cluster of fishermen's hovels near the mouth of the river, along the south bank of which a wharf was built with boulders gathered from the beach. Development proceeded around that wharf, and, small as it was, Leith was already important. The little port was strategically situated, fronting the Forth estuary, and giving ready access to the many little harbours along the east coast of Scotland. Trading was also active across the North Sea to the Low Countries, the Baltic, and the western seaboard of Europe. There were then no constructed roads in Scotland, and no wheeled traffic. Apart from what could be carried by pack horse, transport was by sea, and in all probability it was this situation that first brought the village of North Leith into existence. On that side of the river, opposite the Shore, the craft of shipbuilding developed from very early times.

When men first put to sea their vessels had to be built and repaired, and this work must have been as ancient as Leith itself. Fishermen then did not often venture beyond the Forth estuary, and their boats did not have to be seaworthy. Trading vessels for coastwise voyages were larger, and by the twelfth century Leith mariners were trading with other countries in ships reckoned to be quite adequate for the work. Even so, those were small craft, not many of them much more than fifty tons. Leith yards were normally employed on much smaller ships, but the larger trading vessels would not be beyond their resources. The harbour was tidal, but as the water level between low and high tides was fourteen feet the river offered as much as nine feet of water for launching. Shipbuilding then was necessary and profitable.

The ground behind the yards was taken up by housing for the workers. As there was then no bridge over the river it would be inconvenient to live in South Leith and work in North Leith. Gradually a little colony was established in the north-east corner of the lands attached to the Abbey of the Holy Rood. By the late fifteenth century the Abbot had become aware that this part of his domain was in need of more attention than he had hitherto thought necessary. On the south side of the Water of Leith the de Lestalrics had been succeeded by the Logan family, and the Logans were proving to be thrustful, ambitious people. At the end of the fourteenth century Sir Robert Logan had been given permission by King Robert III to erect Leith to the status of a burgh of barony. One consequence of this was the establishment of various trade incorporations in South Leith. This was followed in 1430 by the building of the little preceptory of St Anthony, occupied by some half dozen canons of that Order invited over from Vienne. These holy men, as the principal source of their income, were granted a quart of wine from every tun landed at Leith, and in addition they organised the auction of wine cargoes in the Vaults of William Logan to the merchants of Edinburgh. Leith's wine trade was growing and prospering. These developments interested and concerned the Abbot of Holyrood, for the Abbey lands at one point extended over the river into South Leith. This was the area known as St Leonard's—not extensive, but becoming evermore valuable and important, as it included the ground between the wine quay and the Vaults. With the increase in trade and the growing importance of Leith as a port, it was highly desirable to have more ready access to the south side of the river, where the Abbey had rents to collect, and where so many changes were taking place. The latest innovation, which must have brought Abbot Ballantyne to the point of decision, was the erection of a very large new church in South Leith adjacent to the preceptory.

This building was begun in 1483, and the work continued for many years thereafter, becoming ever more impressive—and so near to the Abbey lands. The Abbot thought through the situation carefully, and then lost no time in putting his plans into effect. A massive stone bridge was constructed over the river, giving easy access to the St Leonard's lands. At the same time a chapel was built at the north end of the bridge. There already was a chapel in the neighbourhood, barely two hundred yards from the new bridge; but the chapel of St Nicholas was very small, having been provided originally to serve the estimated small needs of that outlying part of the Holyrood lands. The new St Ninian's chapel afforded more accommodation for a population that now seemed certain to grow, and two chaplains were appointed. At the south end of the bridge the Abbot had a tenement erected, and rents from this and other tenants on the St Leonard's lands went to support the two chaplaincies, each of which carried a stipend of fifteen merks per annum. Tolls were taken from those using the bridge and these, together with the offerings made in the chapel, went towards the upkeep of the chapel, bridge, and tenement, any surplus was given to the poor. All these arrangements were confirmed in a charter by King James IV on 1 January 1493. William Maitland in his *History of Edinburgh* quotes a note from this charter: 'If either of the aforesaid Chaplains keep a Lass or Concubine, in an open and notorious Manner, he shall be degraded.' 'This', remarks Maitland, 'seems to imply that they, or either of them, might keep a Miss or Misses, provided it were not publicly known'.

The above charter of 1 January 1493 was drawn up before the new chapel was completed or any chaplains appointed. A charter of mortmain under the Great Seal, dated 18 July 1493 confirmed the arrangements for the maintenance of the two chaplains at St Ninian's, and specified that annual rents from Alexander Broun and Margaret Lindesay his spouse in the St Leonard's lands, from Donald Wrichte in the tenement at the bridge, and another from William Pendreich on the north side of the river would go for the maintenance of the ministry, as it were. From this small beginning, entirely financed locally, the work of the Church in North Leith has continued uninterrupted for five centuries, while the tiny community of the fifteenth century endured and survived immense changes, gradually growing and extending, and offering a unique witness to what might best be described as a communal Christian faith.

On 8 June 1497 King James IV paid a visit to the new chapel of St Ninian's and gave the priest there twenty shillings 'to say ane trentale of messis for the King' and later made a further offering of fourteen shillings. The accounts of the Lord High Treasurer of Scotland, where this payment for thirty masses is listed, refers to the chapel as 'Sanct Rengzanis chapel in Leith', which is a reminder that in the ordinary Scots language of the time 'Ninian' was pronounced 'Ringan', and Leithers knew their little church as 'Sanct Ringan's'.

James IV had a great interest in Leith, for he had an ambition to build a Scots navy, and the shipbuilding centre at that time was North Leith. In 1502 by far the largest ship ever to be built at Leith was ordered for the king. At 600 tons, the new ship took over two and a half years to build, and the workers employed on her boosted the population of the area. Named the *Margaret*, in honour of the daughter of Henry VII of England, whom James married in August 1503, the new ship brought humiliation to all concerned in the work, for at her launching she grounded on the harbour bar and was only refloated after a great deal of work. The king's further shipbuilding plans were pursued at Newhaven.

St Ninian's was fifty years old when the Earl of Hertford sailed into Leith Roads with an English army, landed at

Granton, and spent the next fortnight burning, looting and destroying everything in Leith. The people fled while their goods were stolen or ruined. Nothing was spared; even the wooden pier at the Shore was burned. That was in 1544. Three years later the same man returned, now as Duke of Somerset, and repeated his savagery. Life in the port continued, but on a very low key for many years. The two devastating English raids were followed in 1548 by the occupation of the port by French troops brought over in support of Mary of Guise, mother of Mary Queen of Scots, who acted as Queen Regent during the childhood of her daughter in France. These troops, outnumbering the inhabitants of Leith, camped on the Links adjacent to the village, and in 1559 they built a great wall round the port, taking in the houses on both sides of the river, as well as their own encampment. This was intended to defend Leith, where the Queen Regent had a house. If the opposition of the Protestant party escalated into fighting, Mary had a safe retreat in the port, with access to the sea, if need be.

A wooden bridge was built over the river about 150 yards above the Abbot's bridge, and the great earthen wall continued into North Leith, enclosing St Nicholas' chapel and graveyard. A stone gateway—the St Nicholas port—gave access to the west. The wall then turned sharply north-east along the beach—the short sands as that stretch was known— to the Sand port. About nine months after the erection of this wall, the Queen Regent died in Edinburgh Castle in June 1560, and within a few more weeks the Reformation in Scotland was an accomplished fact. One of the first orders thereafter from the Edinburgh magistrates, was that the town wall of Leith must be demolished, but this was ignored in Leith. Demolition would have been an immense work for a depleted population. The French troops who had built the wall had returned to France, and after the preceding sixteen grim years Leithers were mainly concerned about securing food and shelter in order to stay alive. The wall was left to weather and settle.

The Lords of the Congregation and other leading reformers

acted and spoke as though the country had almost overnight rejected the traditional faith of centuries, in favour of reformed worship. In fact the bulk of the population was slow to adopt the new religion; but there was no persecution, and indeed very little argument. In South Leith the Kirk of Our Lady was designated the parish kirk in place of the collegiate church at Restalrig, and the Preceptory of St Anthony continued to function side by side with the Protestant parish kirk until the later years of the century. In North Leith there seems to have been the same tardy changeover to the reformed faith. It is on record that in 1565 Sir James Dennesoun was chaplain at St Nicholas. It seems incredible that the two chapels of St Nicholas and St Ninian, standing barely a furlong apart, should have been considered necessary for serving that small community, with a chaplain at St Nicholas and two chaplains at St Ninian's. Both chapels must have suffered at the hands of the English in 1544 and 1547, when the whole of Leith was deliberately devastated, and it may be that in the years immediately after the Reformation there were no chaplains at St Ninian's, and the priest at St Nicholas was the sole churchman in North Leith.

This supposition of there being no chaplains at St Ninian's after the Reformation might have been the situation prompting a surprising move by the inhabitants in 1569. The lands hitherto belonging to the Abbey of the Holy Rood had been converted into a temporal lordship under Lord Holyroodhouse, and North Leith was administered by the magistrates of the burgh of Canongate, who granted a feu charter in favour of David Vaus, James Barton and John Wardlaw, indwellers in North Leith, for themselves, and the rest of the inhabitants. This document begins:

> Because of the ardent zeal we have for the preservation and maintaining of the policy and due order among our beloved neighbours, the inhabitants of the town of Leith, on both sides the water thereof within our parish of Holycross; considering likewise that by our office we are

bound, as far as lies in our power, and tending to their advantage to provide for them, as members of our church, and that for the greater promotion of the glory of God, the chapel of St Ninian's underwritten, may be constructed, built and erected by them, with the profit thereof, for the administration of the Word of God, common prayers and sacraments, to the said inhabitants, in all time coming . . .

and so there is now set in feu to the three representatives of the inhabitants of North Leith:

all and sundry chapels, lands, tenements &c. and all others belonging to the said chapels lying within the liberty of the north side of the water of Leith, commonly called Reidside, and particularly the chapel lying there called St Ninian's Chapel, at the bridge-end thereof, easements, commodities, profits &c. to be holden by the said inhabitants &c. of us and our successors, in feu and heritage for ever.

It had become obvious to North Leith landowners, merchants, ship-masters and the like, that two small, semi-ruinous chapels were barely adequate to the spiritual needs of the area so, with both chapels in their possession, the local leaders were free to plan the future. Despite the feu charter, North Leith remained part of the new parish of Holyroodhouse, but the reformers were not likely to discourage anyone building a new church at their own expense. Worship was doubtless continued at St Nicholas, small and ruinous though it was, while St Ninian's was rebuilt on a larger scale to meet the needs of a gradually increasing population.

The project probably took several years to complete. People were desperately poor, and building materials were costly, but labour was no problem. There was no shortage of skill among men who could build ships, and the new St Ninian's, slowly taking shape, was their pride and joy. As happened at St Anthony's Preceptory in South Leith, where the canons, undisturbed, simply grew old and died, James Dennesoun at St Nicholas probably ended his days there and at the new St Ninian's, serving latterly as a reformed minister. It was not uncommon for one-time priests to accept the Reformation, and especially if they could read, write and preach, to continue in office as ministers, for there was a great shortage of suitable parish ministers.

James Dennesoun was succeeded by others, not parish ministers, but visitors, preaching occasionally. The parish kirk was still at Holyrood, but attendance there from North Leith would neither be numerous nor frequent, given the difficulty of the journey. Matters stood thus for some years, until in 1595 Edinburgh presbytery had its attention drawn to the need for a settled minister in North Leith. David Lindsay of South Leith was directed with two other ministers, to visit North Leith and investigate the possibility of 'planting a kirk' there. They reported favourably, but it was not until 1602 that the General Assembly ratified the presbytery's decision to erect North Leith into a parish. The times were difficult for the Church, which was engaged in a struggle with the King who sought to impose an episcopal system of government on the Kirk, despite the deep division between the episcopal and presbyterian factions. Local matters tended to be set aside until a convenient time. From 1602 then, both South Leith and North Leith were in the same situation of being parishes *de facto*, and awaiting Parliamentary sanction to become parishes *de jure*. South Leith had been in this position since 1560 and did not receive the needful act of Parliament until 1609. North Leith, more fortunate, were given legal status for their parish in 1606. The narrative accompanying the act is interesting:

> The inhabitants of the north and south sides of the water and bridge of Leith, being unable to repair to thair parish church of Holyrood, upon thair awin expenses and

charges has biggit to themselffis ane kirk upon the north side of the brig of Leith, and has had ministers serving the cure thereof, and ministering to them the sacraments thir twenty year bygane, therefore his Majesty and the estates of Parliament create and erect the said kirk into a parish kirk to the said inhabitants of the north and south parts of the said Water of Leith, to be called in all time coming the parish kirk of Leith benorth the brigg, and gives and grants to the said parish kirk, and to the haill inhabitants thereof all privileges, freedoms, liberties and immunities belonging to any parish kirk within the kingdom.

In addition to the two chapels, the people of North Leith had at the same time acquired the chaplain's house, the corn tithes of lands in the area, and also the tithes of fish landed at Leith harbour. The new parish was carved out from the extensive parish of Holyrood, and the same Act of 1606 vested the patronage of the new charge in 'the hail of the inhabitants' since the parish kirk had been built by them. This appears to make North Leith parish unique in Scotland. Normally, after the Reformation, the heritors, or local landowners, were reponsible for providing and maintaining the parish kirk and manse and, ideally, a parish school and schoolmaster's house also. It took many years for this ideal to be realised all over the country, but Leith has an outstanding record in this respect. The Kirk of Our Lady in South Leith, designated the parish kirk at the Reformation, was built and maintained by the trade incorporations in the parish: and North Leith, at the same period, provided itself with a kirk through the united efforts of 'the hail of the inhabitants'. So North Leith never suffered the humiliation and frustration endured in many parishes, of having an unacceptable minister nominated to the charge by a patron against whom there was no appeal or redress.

CHAPTER 2

The Struggle to Govern the Kirk

The new parish was tiny. It consisted of the land immediately adjacent to the two chapels of St Nicholas and St Ninian, with the population concentrated in the houses of the fishermen and shipyard workers around the church. To this charge, on 19 September 1599, James Murehead was called and admitted. The date of his birth is unknown, but he graduated Master of Arts at the new University of Edinburgh in July 1598, and if he was then twenty years old that would be quite mature for a student in those days. On the other hand, by the time of his graduation he had already married twice, which would suggest he was rather older. He first married a Miss Paterson who must have died soon thereafter. His second marriage was on 15 December 1596, almost three years before he graduated. This time his bride was Janet Dennistoun, who survived her husband. Her name is intriguing. There could not have been many Dennistouns around, and the priest at St Nicholas' Chapel for some years after the Reformation was James Dennesoun, which was presumably the same name. In the Reformed Kirk there was no rule of celibacy for ministers, and no bar to James Dennesoun marrying. If he married and had a daughter she could have been of marriageable age by 1596, and her marriage to a divinity student would pave the way for his being called to the new charge where her father had served.

Little is known about James Murehead, but that little is interesting. While he was minister of North Leith, a member of Edinburgh Presbytery, and of the Synod of Lothian, King James VI fell heir to the throne of England on the death of Queen Elizabeth in 1603. His Majesty forthwith began preparations for the journey to London, and the ministers of the Church in Scotland were very perturbed. James favoured episcopal government for the Scottish Church, with himself as head, after the English pattern. This was not widely favoured in Scotland, the weight of opinion preferring the presbyterian system. A number of specific points had been put to James, who was reluctant to give any clear answers, and this hurried departure south provided an opportunity of shelving consideration of these matters indefinitely.

On Tuesday 5 April 1603 the Synod of Lothian was in session at Haddington when word was brought that his Majesty had that morning set out for England. David Calderwood the Church historian wrote that when the news reached the synod meeting 'they dissolved in haste to meet the King. They mett him above Hadintoun, all on their knees, and prayed for him'. This conjures up rather an entertaining picture for the twentieth century reader, who may imagine James and his entourage reaching that point on the A1 road where the Haddington by-pass branches off. There the cavalcade was halted as the entire membership of the Synod of Lothian were found on their knees praying for the King! But the ministers got no satisfaction. King James had no intention of making any promises, especially when his mind was so taken up with other affairs of state. So the synod chose six of their number to seek an audience with his Majesty, and to raise certain urgent issues with him:

1. The suppressing of Papists in his absence and the preservation of discipline. 2. For order touching stipends. 3. For reliefe of good brethrein of the ministrie of England. 4. For libertie to the warded and distressed brethrein of the ministrie of Scotland.

The chosen six were Mr Robert Wallace, Mr James Carmichael, Mr Archibald Oswald, Mr Henrie Blyth, Mr Michael Cranstoun and Mr James Murehead. The choice of the North Leith minister draws attention to the fact that in South Leith the minister, Mr David Lindsay, was a close friend of the King, and indeed was one of those travelling south with him that day. Lindsay favoured the episcopal form of Church government, and had recently been nominated Bishop of Ross. From the safer distance of Whitehall, King James made further moves towards the introduction of Episcopacy to the Scottish Church, and on 1 July 1606 a protest against this was signed by a number of Scots ministers. James Murehead was the only member of Edinburgh presbytery signing that protest.

Congregational life in the early seventeenth century bore little resemblance to anything known in the church today. The kirk itself was barely more than four walls and a roof. There was a pulpit, but no floor and no pews. As the kirk was the only place in the village where people could meet under shelter, a great deal went on there that was not religious. In May 1606 for example the session forbad the use of the kirk any longer for sailmaking and repairing. As no one then possessed clocks or watches the kirk bell was of public importance, and the bellringer a responsible official, ringing the morning bell at five am and the curfew at eight in the evening. Even so there was little idea of punctuality, and the session had to ask the minister to make an intimation urging people to come to the kirk on time. There were regular services on Sundays and Thursdays, when the minister preached, and morning and evening prayers on other days. Only the Sunday service was compulsory, and the elders actively sought out those absenting themselves. They were not always politely received. David Gourlay was found lying in bed during the service. He threatened to throw the elder downstairs and was brought before the session, when he promised not to do it again, and was warned that another long lie on Sunday would cost him five pounds!

Sabbath breakers were always accused of committing their misdeeds 'in tyme of sermon', whether the miscreant was cutting kale or playing golf. What people did on Sunday evenings never seems to have been questioned. Golfing was a frequent offence, but in June 1611 two men were brought to the session for playing football 'in tyme of sermon'. The stool of repentance, where those convicted of various offences sat to serve at least part of their sentence, was always referred to as 'the pillar', presumably because the stool was set against a pillar.

An interesting case in January 1611 was that of a man caught on Sunday catching rabbits on the Links with the aid of a ferret and a net. This is a reminder that the Links was once a happy hunting ground for rabbits, and for long a popular name for the Links was 'the coney warren' ('coney' being the old word for a rabbit). By the end of the seventeenth century famine and dire poverty had taken such toll over the years that all the rabbits on the Links had been caught and eaten, and the old name was forgotten.

There was no police establishment and community life was rough and ready. The kirk session dealt with petty offenders, but graver crimes were supposedly dealt with by a magistrate. A constant complaint however, was that there was no resident magistrate, and rarely did any magistrate visit North Leith. The tolbooth and the jougs were frequent forms of punishment, but to a large extent people sought to settle wrongs in their own way. Most people were illiterate, but Mr Murehead was fortunate in having a young man, Moses Wardrop as his Reader, Session Clerk, Precentor and Schoolmaster. A man of many parts, Moses remained active for many years, serving with a succession of ministers. Mr Murehead, being a man of his time, understood his congregation and was highly respected and esteemed. For all that he was more than once physically assaulted and slandered—which annoyed the session but did not shock the elders as it would today. The minister also complained that far too often he was not informed of sickness until death frustrated any effort at pastoral care. The centuries have not made much difference here. The expectation of life was then very short, but on 16 July 1607 the kirk session approved a gift of 20/– to Allan Dowgelsone, 'a poor man, being of the age of 108'!

Having served his parish well, and done his bit for the advancement of the Presbyterian cause Mr Murehead died 'in his upper chalmer at sevin houris in the morning of 29 October 1612.' His three sisters, Agnes, Margaret and Grisell, all married to ministers, were named as executrices of his will.

There followed rather a long vacancy before David Forrester was inducted to the charge on 16 December 1613. He was a deceptively mild-mannered man who none the less was possessed of strong presbyterian principles. He came to the work at North Leith when the Church in Scotland was increasingly irked by King James's determination to bring it under episcopal discipline. The Five Articles of Perth in 1617 ordered the people to kneel at Communion, instituted the private celebration of Baptism and the Lord's Supper, the observation of the Christian Year, and the rite of Confirmation. A General Assembly at St Andrews in November of that year rejected these Articles, and the king, furious, proceeded to impose them on the unwilling Church. Despite widespread opposition, it seems that only about a dozen ministers were actually deprived for their obstinacy in rejecting the Articles. David Forrester of North Leith was suspended by the Court of High Commission on 2 July 1619 and confined to Aberdeen. He continued his opposition there and was again summoned before the Commission on 25 November that year 'for administering the Communion in a manner not in accordance with the prescribed order'. He was turned over to Patrick Forbes, Bishop of Aberdeen to be dealt with. Forbes, however, was so impressed by Forrester that he simply translated him from North Leith to the parish of Rathven in Moray, remarking of Forrester that 'though he stood on his own conscience, he is as modest and subject to hear reason as the youngest scholar in Scotland'.

The Church of Scotland was now episcopalian in its government, by the imposition of the royal will, and the vacancy at North Leith was quickly supplied by the appointment of Henry Charteris, who was admitted to the charge by the Archbishop of St Andrews in April 1620. This was a surprising induction to the new little parish of North Leith, for Charteris was a prominent churchman. He had been one of the original students when Edinburgh University opened in 1583, and he graduated MA in 1587. For twenty years before the North Leith vacancy Charteris had been Principal of Edinburgh University and Professor of Divinity; but the University was the 'Toun's College', and the town council had a considerable say in the affairs of the University. Principal Charteris fell out with the town council and resigned his academic chair, quickly accepting the call to North Leith. Both sides in this dispute had been too sensitive and too hasty. At the beginning of 1627 Charteris returned to his university chair, but he died the following July. It was said of him that 'he was certainly one of the most learned men of his time, both in the tongues and in philosophy and divinity'. Once again the vacancy at North Leith was short: after only a few weeks David Forrester was recalled by the elders, deacons and inhabitants, and with consent of the archbishop was readmitted on 20 September 1627. It says much for Forrester's character and personality that this should have happened, but the move was only effected, it was said, through Mrs Forrester. She was a cousin of Sir William Alexander of Menstrie, later Earl of Stirling, who persuaded the people of Rathven to agree to their minister's return to Leith.

Three years later Mr Forrester had the satisfaction of having his little parish extended to twenty times its original size. In 1630 the baronies of Hillhousefield and Newhaven were detached from the parish of St Cuthbert's and added to North Leith. No doubt this had been the original intention when North Leith parish was first formed under the Act of 1606. The area then designated as North Leith came from the parish of Holyrood. The extensive additions now made also brought the corn tithes of the land and the fish tithes of Newhaven. It was assumed at the time that this new annexation was *quoad sacra*, and the heritors of Hillhousefield and Newhaven continued to contribute to the stipend of the minister of St Cuthbert's. It was not until 1802, in the course of a legal process of augmentation pursued by the minister of North Leith, that it was pointed out that the annexation of 1630 was *quoad omnia*, and that what had been paid to the St Cuthbert's minister ought in fact to go to the minister of North Leith.

The parish that was now so largely extended had only existed as a parish for less than thirty years, but the community was centuries old. There was no long tradition of congregational life. The Church was in a missionary situation in which its effectiveness to a large degree depended on the life and example of the elders. Supersitition was rife, pre-Christian attitudes and habits still counted for much in the lives of the people. Office-bearers in the Kirk had an unending struggle to achieve and maintain higher standards of morality, better self-discipline, and a grasp of what were deemed the essentials of Christian faith. Agnes Dunlop tried to murder her brother, stabbing him with a knife. He survived, but there was no magistrate to conduct a trial. The session sentenced her to the cockstool, where she had to remain with the knife in her hand for all to witness. But the elders did not hesitate to adopt a tough stance, when all else failed. Margaret Quhippo was brought up for fornication, and the session had her put in the jougs. They also discovered that she did not belong to North Leith, so they ordained that when she came out of the jougs she was to be banished from the parish and told that if ever she reappeared in North Leith she would be drowned, as she was known to be a thief and a whore.

There was never any knowing what people might think of next. In 1622 a young couple had themselves proclaimed as intending to marry. When it came to the bit however they didn't bother the minister; instead they went along to evening prayers, and thereafter married each other in the presence of some friends. This form of marriage had always been legal in Scotland, although irregular. They thought they had saved themselves the usual marriage fees, but the session accused them of 'scorning the ordinance of God'. They had to make public repentance and pay the proper fees after all. In 1627 David Forrester lost patience with couples coming for marriage, who apparently had not the haziest idea of what Christianity was about, and he then made a rule that anyone seeking marriage must be able to repeat the Lord's Prayer, the belief (ie the creed) and the Ten Commandments. Failing that they would have to pay forty shillings to the poor box.

Church attendance remained one of the main areas of Kirk discipline. There were always recalcitrants who were prepared as it were to cock a snook at the kirk session, but they were few in the parish. No one could leave the parish to seek work elsewhere without a certificate of character, and no widow or pauper would receive help when there were always far more in need than could be served from the poor box. The 'deserving poor' always came first. So the elders were always assiduous in rounding up for the kirk everyone except the aged and infirm. During his first pastorate in North Leith, however, in 1616, David Forrester, with the agreement of the session, intimated that in future no one was to bring young bairns to the kirk 'as they trouble the hearers of the Word, especially upon the Lord's day'. The atmosphere of peace and goodwill normal to a twentieth century church service is the result of generations of striving to that end. Before the celebration of the Lord's Supper in North Leith in the early seventeenth century the elders were sent round their districts, not to distribute communion cards, but to enquire into the relationships of members with their families and neighbours, and to try to effect reconciliation, where there was strife, before coming forward to communion. Another practice in church which the minister found irritating was when women who brought their stools to sit on almost always set them against the walls. Intimation was made urging them to bring their seats forward into the body of the kirk. The men could be equally annoying. They generally stood, but they didn't stand in one place, but moved around talking to neighbours, even after the service was in progress. It took a forceful preacher to hold the attention of that kind of congregation.

Life for most people in seventeenth century Scotland was short, usually uncomfortable and often dangerous. Death was so frequent that something of a callous attitude was adopted as a protection for inward grief. Wakes were common, but there was normally no funeral service, since the dead were beyond the range of human help. Witchcraft was a constant concern, and accusations were made before the session from time to time. In 1630 Majorie Cuninghame, Bessie Hogg and Catherine Lasone were all burnt as witches. Much has been written about the plague in 1645 – the last such visitation in the port when most of the population died. But plague had always been a threat, and many outbreaks took place in earlier times. There were two serious epidemics in the winters of 1605–6 and 1624–5. The bellringer was then busy with the passing bell, tolling for the dead. But the desperate state of many of the living had also to be remembered, and the session decided that the passing bell would only be rung when relatives of the deceased paid 12/- to the poor box. The parish poor were to continue as a great responsibility and problem for many years, and all kinds of fines and fees were introduced to help build up the poor fund. The elders themselves did not escape: in 1623 it was decided to fine those who failed to attend meetings without sufficient excuse, or who arrived late.

The addition of Newhaven to the parish was very welcome, but the people of that village were kittle cattle. Edinburgh had bought Newhaven from King James IV in 1510, but the Newhaveners did not in any way consider themselves as belonging to Edinburgh. That did not disturb North Leith folk, who shared that view of Edinburgh as a place apart. It was very soon evident however, that the Newhaveners were not prepared to be called Leithers either, and this was to cause problems in years to come. The Free Fishermen's Society, a strong and influential body even then, stipulated that they would not consent to being joined to North Leith unless they were allowed to look after their own poor. The North Leith elders readily agreed to the Fishermen's demand. In the Reformed Church the kirk session was responsible for the local poor, and the Newhaveners' attitude looked like a generous shouldering of a heavy responsibility. The Fishermen however, then made it plain that caring for their own poor should free them from the duty of contributing to the poor of North Leith. In fact they were not prepared to put any offerings in the plate at the door of North Leith Church: instead the Free Fishermen on Sundays put a collection plate on a stand beside the road leading from Newhaven to North Leith, where churchgoers could make their contributions and be sure that the money would not leave Newhaven. Knowing Newhaven, the North Leith kirk session agreed to this without comment. Mr Forrester might have made an issue of the matter, but he was a diplomat, and there was no trouble.

David Forrester died in 1633, and there was a long vacancy. Strong and growing opposition to episcopal government in the Scottish Kirk was leading to tension and trouble in many places. In the neighbouring parish of South Leith both the ministers were Episcopalian in sympathy, but most of the congregation was at odds with them, and the laird, Lord Balmerino, was one of the leaders of the Covenanting party. North Leith, from its inception as a parish, had had no trouble of this kind, as both David Forrester and Henry Charteris, even under episcopalian rule, had been well liked in the parish.

David Robertson, editor of the published *South Leith Records*, when commenting on a visit made to that parish by the Bishop of Edinburgh in 1672, says that the bishop, George Wishart, had many years before been minister of North Leith, but had been deposed on his refusing to sign the Covenant. This is an error. George Wishart was never minister of North Leith. He served in St Andrews and later at Newcastle. He had many adventures and was imprisoned more than once before being consecrated Bishop of Edinburgh in 1662. He died in 1671, so it was his successor who visited South Leith in 1672.

The North Leith vacancy was filled in 1636 when Andrew Fairfoul was translated from Leslie in Fife. Five years later King Charles I presented Fairfoul to North Leith. This very odd presentation of a minister to a charge where he had already been serving as minister for five years can only be explained on the assumption that the 'elders, deacons and haill inhabitants' of North Leith had called Mr Fairfoul to be their minister despite episcopal rule in the Kirk. The scanty records of this period offer no explanation. Presumably Mr Fairfoul would not be officially recognised as minister in North Leith until his presentation, but this probably made no difference locally. The five years between his translation to Leith in 1636 and his presentation in 1641 cover the period of the National Covenant and the overthrow of episcopalianism in the Kirk. Andrew Fairfoul remained in Leith till 1652 when he was translated to Duns, and after the Restoration and the renewal of episcopacy in Scotland, Fairfoul, nominated by King Charles II, was consecrated Archbishop of Glasgow in 1661, and died two years later.

During his sixteen years at North Leith Mr Fairfoul does not seem to have made any great personal impact, but for Leith it was a time of much excitement and much suffering. The National Covenant, or 'Confession of Faith' as it was popularly known, was originally drawn up by Archibald Johnston of Warriston and Alexander Henderson on 23 February 1638. It was revised by some of the leading nobles opposing Charles I. On 27 February it was read to some hundreds of ministers in the Tailors' Hall in Edinburgh, and next day to a meeting of barons and gentlemen. Then at 4 pm on the last day of February it was taken to Greyfriars Church and signed by the nobles, barons and gentlemen. That night Warriston wrote four copies on parchment, and next morning almost three hundred ministers signed at Taylors' Hall. In the days following, hundreds of copies were written and distributed to the parishes. All those admitted to communion were invited to sign, and those who could not write signed through a notary. Normally only men signed, but women were not debarred, and some did sign. Copies were written on sheepskin parchments, and not many have survived, but the copy signed in North Leith and Newhaven is preserved in New College Library. It is dated 'At the north kirk of Leith 7 and 15 April 1638' and the list is headed by the signatures of eight nobles, the rest of the names being those of parishioners.

Communications then were slow, and it took many months for copies to reach the more remote areas. The General Assembly sat in Glasgow in December 1638 and voted in favour of an addendum to the Covenant. This emphasised certain points which had either been omitted in the original document, or were considered ambiguous: the Five Articles of Perth, the office of bishop, and the holding of civil offices by churchmen were all to be rejected. This addendum came to be known as the Glasgow Determination, and all ministers, university and school teachers, and others who had not yet signed, were told to make sure that the Glasgow Determination prefixed their signatures. In places where the Covenant had already been signed the Glasgow Determination was to be inserted above the signatures. This in fact was done on the North Leith copy, which had been signed within six weeks of the original drawing up of the document. Many of the signatures are illegible, but the following names are clearly written, and will no doubt be of interest to their twentieth century descendants. Most of these family names are still common enough in Leith:

William Rammag	Robert Davidsone	Andrew Maine
Arthour Gib	James Dougall	David West
Alexander Broun	James Fforrester	Johne Anderson
Johne Thomsone	Georg Thomson	Thomas Andersone
Robert Hendersone	Robert Welshe	Johne Crookes
David Gourlay	Thomas Moubray	Alexr Young
Robert Ker	James Ker	Alexander Sandersone
Thomas Muddie	Williame Henrie	Williame Coustone
Georg Willsone	Thomas Matheson	Adame Brand
James Pittillo	George Caird	Robert Ramsay
Ja. Sinclare	Wm. Sinclair	William Broune
James Duncane	Patrik Mitcheill	James Tosh

There were no spelling rules then, and the names are set out as they appear on the parchment. The signing was not completed on the 7th and 15th of April, as the dating on the parchment suggests. There is a record note that the kirk session 'concludit that the covenant sall be bought and sall be read upon sonday the xxii day of apryle and that all men sould hauld up ther hands and sweir to the samyn and thairefter subscryve the said covenant'. The signing of the National Covenant was followed by a period of Presbyterian ascendancy, and in the following month, in preparation for celebrating the Lord's Supper in the Presbyterian way, three hundred 'tickets' were ordered for the congregation. Communion tokens only date from the Presbyterian establishment in 1690. From the Reformation until that date communion tickets were issued—small pieces of parchment to be handed in as is done today with communion cards.

The English Civil War elicited in Scotland strong support for the Parliamentary party, as it was reckoned that the best hope for a Presbyterian Kirk lay with that side. In South Leith the two Episcopalian ministers of the 1630s had gone—one simply disappeared and the other was deposed. They were succeeded by strong Presbyterians, and intimation was made from the pulpit that able-bodied men would be welcome in the Army of the Covenant. In North Leith, with the Episcopalian Andrew Fairfoul in charge, there was no such encouragement from the pulpit.

Fairfoul's Episcopalianism counted for little in the daily life of the people, and not even in Sunday worship. The difference between Presbyterian and Episcopalian was an argument about Church government; the manner of worship was largely unaffected, and even the ecclesiastical argument faded into the background in Leith, where people were much more concerned with trying to stay alive. By far the most serious outbreak of bubonic plague the port had ever known took place in 1645, when from May till November the epidemic carried off almost two-thirds of the population. The plague was followed by famine, for no harvest had been gathered in

1645, and few of the survivors were strong enough to till the land in the spring of 1646. Recovery from those years was slow, and soon there was new excitement as the Covenanting army was paraded on the Links, awaiting the arrival of Cromwell's Ironsides. Allegiances had changed since the English beheaded their king in 1649. Scotland was shocked, and feeling now ran strongly for King Charles II who, under pressure, agreed to support the Covenant. Sandy Leslie, a wee man with a big reputation gained from fighting in the Low Countries, commanded the covenanting army, and kept his waiting troops occupied building a mile-long rampart and ditch from the St Anthony port in the old town wall southward to the Calton. This was to become Leith Walk, but the English army did not arrive, so General Leslie marched south and was soundly defeated at the Battle of Dunbar in September 1650. This was an event of immense significance for North Leith, since following the battle the English army rode into Edinburgh and at once occupied Leith.

Mindful of the stories that had come down to them of the English destruction of Leith a century before, the arrival of the Commonwealth soldiers was viewed with the utmost apprehension. Cromwell himself left almost at once, leaving the troops under the command of General Monck. The common soldiers were soon settled in a permanent camp on the Links, and the officers were quartered in private houses, where the reluctant householders had to accept what they could not refuse. Every available accommodation was now taken up by the occupying force. Their valuable horses had to be stabled; armoury and ammunition could not be left to rust; stores and equipment were bulky and needed protection from the weather. All this mostly affected South Leith, as there was no accommodation on the north side, apart from some private houses, which were of course taken for quarters. But before long it became apparent to Leithers that this new breed of Englishmen was a totally different kind of invader from the savages of the 1540s. These were disciplined men. They were rough and tough, as was to be expected, but they were not needlessly violent. Their officers were strict and even harsh, but they were fair and reasonable, so long as it was understood that military exigency must always come first. South Leith church was at once requisitioned and the congregation driven to worship on the Links in summer and at the old ruinous kirk of Restalrig when winter set in.

North Leith church was not interfered with, but there was plenty disturbance. Leith was under military rule, and the occupying force was set to work rebuilding the old town wall which had crumbled considerably during the century of its existence. This was very much against the wishes of the Edinburgh magistrates, but they could not prevent it. Once the wall was repaired all movement in and out of Leith was strictly monitored. Each of the ports was manned by a sentry so that all exits and entrances were controlled. When work on the wall was completed there was not much for the troops to do, and they became restive. In September 1652 trouble broke out when twelve pence weekly was deducted from the soldiers' pay to provide a fund for a store. A group of the men rebelled, and four of the most prominent were arrested, court-martialled, and condemned to be hanged. On appeal the death sentence was restricted to one man, as a warning to others. The victim was decided by drawing lots, and the lot fell on the man acknowledged to have been the ringleader. When the day for the execution arrived 'all the women of this town joyned together in a petition to save his life, which was accordingly granted'.

A few months later, in 1653, Cromwell ordered the building of a citadel, where the troops could be garrisoned. This was a very large undertaking, generally welcomed in Leith. Edinburgh town council was obliged to contribute £5000 for this work. In Leith the townsfolk looked forward to the time when their lodgers would be able to go and occupy their own quarters, and in the meantime there was the prospect of much paid work for carters and various skilled tradesmen. The people of the port, indeed, after some months of nervous apprehension, settled down very well with the English newcomers, and several local girls married soldiers.

There could be no ignoring military requirements however. It was decided to erect the Citadel in North Leith, inside the protecting wall. The site chosen was one calculated to cause the least disturbance. The corner taken up by the old St Nicholas Chapel and graveyard was ideal, as no houses stood there; but the loss of the burial ground was a serious blow. It was quickly agreed with the South Leith people that North Leith burials would be accommodated in South Leith churchyard until some other arrangement could be made.

Andrew Fairfoul had departed for Duns in 1652, and his successor, John Knox was ordained to North Leith the following year. He was a man very different from Fairfoul. Strongly Presbyterian, Knox had graduated MA at Edinburgh University in 1641. As a probationer he joined the army of the Covenant, and became chaplain to Sir John Brown's Regiment of Horse. He was at the battle of Inverkeithing in July 1651 when Cromwell's troops defeated the Scots supporting Charles II. After that he had a spell as chaplain to the Earl of Angus. His coming to North Leith in 1653 was matched by the arrival of John Hog to the first charge at South Leith, the second charge there remaining vacant throughout the occupation. These two ministers had similar views, and appear to have got along very well together in their neighbouring parishes. But neither of them was *persona grata* with the English troops, as they were fervent supporters of Charles II.

Work on the Citadel progressed steadily, and as parts of the building were completed, stores, equipment and horses were gradually moved there from the various buildings that had been commandeered. The congregation of South Leith church were able to return to that building in November 1654 to resume normal Sunday worship but John Hog the minister, foolishly insisted on praying in public for King Charles II, and brought fresh trouble on himself and his congregation.

General Monck, foreseeing a long stay in Leith, encouraged

English families to come and settle in the port. Some were the families of soldiers under his command, others were small-time entrepreneurs or people with special skills, who could benefit the community. A number of these folk now began attending South Leith Church, and others, quartered in the Citadel, made their way to St Ninian's Kirk in North Leith. Monck from his first coming had shown himself sympathetic to Leith in the port's sense of oppression under Edinburgh's irksome rule; but the General was serving in the army of Cromwell, the Lord Protector, and was bound to take note of a local minister praying for King Charles. He could have had Mr Hog arrested; instead he ordered him to hand back the keys of his church, which was closed again at the beginning of May. It was also common knowledge that Mr Knox in North Leith was of like mind with Mr Hog. The order for closing the church came from Timothy Wilks, the Deputy Governor of the Citadel. He forbad any Scots minister to preach in church until further notice. So John Knox found his church barred to him also. As some of the garrison had been attending the parish church he moved to the Citadel and held services there—presumably in the open air, as the Citadel was still far from complete. This arrangement was not acceptable to the Deputy Governor however, so public worship for the parish was moved to Newhaven, where the ruins of the old St James's Chapel could still provide some shelter from the wind.

It took a long time to resolve this impasse. While the North Leith congregation worshipped at Newhaven the South Leith folk had to be content with the Links until the autumn, when they moved to Restalrig. A petition to the Deputy Governor for forgiveness and a return to the church got no answer, so Cromwell himself was written to at the beginning of 1656. The reply to this came in June. It was a conciliatory letter, directing that, for the time being both North and South Leith congregations should worship together in North Leith Church, until such time as all stores and equipment could be moved to the Citadel and all argument about the use of premises would cease. This joint worship commenced on 10 July 1656 and continued for a year, during which an effort was made to restore some of the damage done to South Leith Kirk by the occupation. The last of the joint services in North Leith was held on 14 June 1657 and on the following Friday George Kintore was inducted to South Leith second charge. That event, marking also the return to the church of South Leith, was celebrated by a dinner to the Presbytery—perhaps the first induction dinner in the Scottish Church.

The garrison at the Citadel, perhaps not favourably impressed by the Scots Kirk, in view of the various arguments and ejections from kirks they had been witnessing, set up their own church in the Citadel, and resorted there for worship. It was a Baptist chapel—a branch of the Church unknown to Leithers. It had a short life, for it did not survive the departure of the occupying troops after the death of Cromwell.

The Citadel, completed, was an impressive building. John Ray, the English naturalist, visited Leith in 1661 and described the Citadel as 'one of the best fortifications that we ever beheld, passing fair and sumptuous'. Within the freestone walls he detailed:

> very pleasant, convenient and well-built houses for the governor, officers and soldiers, and for magazines and stores. There is also a good, capacious chapel, the piazza, or void space within, as large as Trinity College (Cambridge) great court ... The building cost ... above £100,000 sterling. Indeed I do not see how it could cost less; in England it would have cost much more.

English families who had been induced to settle in Leith during the occupation, did not leave again with the troops. Involved in various lines of business they remained as parishioners. The high hopes that the restoration of King Charles II would see presbyterianism established as the Scottish form of religion, were quickly dashed. Charles had never had any intention of keeping his promise to support the

Covenant—a promise which, he would claim, had been given under duress. Episcopalianism now became the order of the day and the Presbyterians could only remember Psalm 146— 'Put not your trust in princes . . . in whom there is no help.'

The Restoration brought no joy to the Covenanters, but it did encourage a spirit of hope and optimism in the country. In Leith a number of small manufactories were set up, most of which did not long survive. For some years the Citadel was a centre of industry. A printing press had been installed there. The machine came to Leith with the occupying troops, and was set going before the Citadel had been begun. General Monck had the idea of keeping his troops in touch with affairs back home, and the press was operated by Christopher Higgins and a team of Englishmen, who reprinted a London newspaper called *A diurnal of some passages and affairs.* This was a shortlived effort, as was the printing of *Mercurius Scotisus—true character of affairs in England, Scotland, Ireland and other foreign parts, collected for publique satisfaction.* When the troops withdrew, the press remained, and at the end of 1660 there appeared from it the first genuinely Scottish newspaper, the *Mercurius Caledonius*—the forerunner of what emerged in the eighteenth century as the *Caledonian Mercury.*

Another enterprise at the Citadel was the setting up of a glasswork by Robert Pape in 1663. He was probably one of the English settlers, and knowledge of his enterprise comes to us from an advertisement in the *Kingdom's Intelligencer,* another small newspaper printed at the Citadel press:

A Remarkable Advertisement to the Country and Strangers. That there is a Glass-house erected in the Citadel of Leith, where all sorts and quantities of glass are made and sould at the prices following: to wit, the wine glass at three shillings two boddels, the beer glass at two shillings sixpence; the quart bottel at eighteen shillings, the pynt bottel at nine shilling, the chopin bottel at four shillings sixpence, the muskin bottel at two shillings sixpence, all Scots money, and so forth of all sorts, conform to the proportion of the glasses; better stuff and stronger than imported.

William Hutchison in his *Tales and Traditions of Leith* pointed out that this appears to be the first mention of beer in Scotland, where the common drink was ale, and muskins (mutchkins) and chopins were unknown in England. Pape's business did not survive more than about a dozen years, the final blow falling when the cashier absconded with a large sum of money. The glasswork continued under a succession of owners, lingering on well into the next century, struggling to make a profit against stiff English opposition. In seventeenth century Leith there was a chronic lack of capital, and no skilled workers for what was a highly skilled craft.

Edinburgh had been compelled to contribute £5000 towards the cost of building the Citadel, and at the Restoration the whole costly structure was ordered to be demolished. The city saw no benefit, and only considerable expense in maintaining such a fortress. Charles II however had made a gift of the Citadel area to the Earl of Lauderdale, his minister in Scotland. Not only so, but Charles, together with the gift, issued a royal charter erecting North Leith into a free burgh of regality, with a weekly market, a yearly fair, and all the other rights and privileges normally belonging to such a free burgh. From time to time it has been maintained that while Edinburgh certainly came into possession of the superiority of South Leith, North Leith was a separate burgh, over which the city had no authority. This is a misunderstanding. What happened was that the Earl of Lauderdale informed Edinburgh of North Leith's new status as a burgh of regality, where independent trade incorporations might be established, a weekly market held, and an annual fair. The Edinburgh magistrates, appalled at the damage this could do to the city's business, agreed to buy North Leith from the Earl, and paid what was later described as the exorbitant price of £6000 sterling. This effectively prevented North Leith's burgh status ever being publicly declared, or any of the accompanying privileges being exercised. The trades in North Leith remained part of the trades of the burgh of Canongate. There is no record, however, of the charter ever having been cancelled. At the time the new burgh of North Leith was given the name of Charlestoun, but, once Edinburgh had acquired possession, that was ignored.

The coast between the Water of Leith and Newhaven has always suffered much from erosion. Before long the Citadel wall along the beach from the St Nicholas port to the Sand port was undermined by the sea and partially collapsed. The houses within the wall remained intact however, and the chapel, with no congregation to maintain it, was pulled down, and its internal fittings were purchased by the Governors of Heriot's Hospital for the refurbishment of their own chapel. The Citadel area then became a favoured district for several families of the Scottish aristocracy. The Duke of Gordon, Lady Bruce, Sir William Erskine, Lady Eleanor Douglas and others had houses there till well into the eighteenth century. From the late seventeenth century moreover, the Citadel became a resort of sea-bathers, and houses there were offered for rent to citizens looking for salubrious summer quarters adjacent to the sea and free from the stinks and cramped accommodation of the old city.

John Knox was still minister of North Leith at the time of the Restoration but, being irreconcilably Presbyterian, he was deprived in 1662. It was hinted to him that if he went to London and spoke to the right people it would probably not be too difficult to be presented to another charge in some place rather more remote than Leith. He refused this advice, so had to accept the hardship of unemployment. The following year he was succeeded at North Leith by James Reid, who has remained a shadowy figure, apparently making little impact on the community during the eight years he remained in the charge before his death in 1671. He was, of course, Episcopalian—a north country man, graduating at King's College, Aberdeen in 1652. Aberdeen was an Episcopalian stronghold, and after a spell at school-mastering Reid became minister of the second charge at Kirkwall before being presented to North Leith when just over thirty years of age. While he acquiesced in the Episcopalian style of church government, Reid was no fool. He discovered that when the Citadel was built, the ground acquired for that purpose had included part of the North Leith glebe. The minister therefore presented a claim to the city magistrates for the return of the ground, or else for suitable compensation. On 5 January 1666, at a meeting of the bailies, council and deacons of crafts:

> Upon the petition of Mr James Reid, minister of North Leith, bearing that the glebe of that church being taken away to the citadel of Leith, and craving that the council would be pleased to make up the same, the council, out of favor, although they find themselves noways bound in law to do the same, have remitted to the water bailie of Leith, and the baron bailie of the Canongate, that they cause measure off so much land as will correspond to the former glebe.

Meanwhile, the inconvenience for North Leith people of having to bury their dead in South Leith churchyard had not been overlooked, and in December 1663 a committee of Edinburgh town council visited the Citadel and the surrounding area to find a suitable place for a new graveyard. Early in 1664 the inhabitants of North Leith were presented with:

> a Piece of Garden Ground on the south side of their antient Cemitery and Hospital of the Length of 50 Ells on the south side, 55 on the north side, 54 on the east side, and 23 on the west side in Breadth.

For the next two and a half centuries the dead of North Leith were buried in this ground beside the river.

When Mr Reid died in 1671, the 'elders, deacons and

inhabitants' presented Thomas Wilkie to the charge in December of that year. This could only be done with the consent of the Archbishop of St Andrews, and this took time. Mr Wilkie was formally installed on 4 June 1672. His ministry was marked by the rebuilding and extension of the church, when the famous Dutch-style steeple was introduced, bearing the date 1675. Alexander Kincaid in his *History of Edinburgh* describes that building:

> It measures 100 ft by 60 ft over the walls, and is very neatly finished within. It has a gallery that goes roun three sides of it, and on the front it is decorated with the various devices belonging to the societies in Leith. Above this, at each end, is another. The north side of the present church was a part of St. Ninian's Chapel, and in the neighbourhood, in St. Nicholas' Wynd, was the parish school.

It was probably at this time of reconstruction and refurbishment of the church that a flagstone floor was first laid. This amenity was generally being introduced in churches in the later seventeenth century. Until that time, with nothing but the bare earth underfoot, it was common practice to bury important people under the floor. The General Assembly from about 1640 repeatedly ruled against this unhygienic practice, but the long established tradition was abandoned with great reluctance. When the old parish kirk had finally ceased to be a place of worship, work was put in hand in 1826 to convert the building to commercial use, and when the ground was excavated near the spot where the old pulpit had stood, two skeletons were dug up. It would be a fair presumption that these were the remains of James Murehead and David Forrester, the first two ministers of North Leith parish kirk, who died in the manse in 1612 and 1633 respectively. It was the early practice to bury the minister beside the pulpit. This was done in South Leith for David Lindsay in 1613, and in the adjacent parish the same practice was no doubt followed.

It was in this newly reconstructed kirk with its innovative steeple that there occurred during divine service an event that caused such an upset that it was remembered and talked about to the third and fourth generation following.

There was then in Leith a body of Quakers, who were not numerous, but they were vocal, expressing opinions at odds with the Presbyterian view of religion. George Fox's Society of Friends were first called Quakers at Derby in 1650, and perhaps his influence reached Leith through the English troops occupying the port at that period. The Baptist church faded after the soldiers had gone, but Quakerism seems to have taken root. Their leader was Hector Allan, a shipmaster, who held regular meetings in his house in North Leith. The Society of Friends had no use for the Church establishment, nor for an ordained ministry, and while they were pacifist in principle, they made no effort to conceal or play down their ideas. Whatever was said at the meetings in Hector Allan's house was soon public knowledge in the village, so that Quaker tenets became a kind of scandal.

At last the minister, Mr Wilkie, decided to take a stand in the matter, and in his sermon on Sunday 31 March 1678 he made pointed reference to the local Quakers, denouncing their odd ideas. Hector Allan did not normally attend church, but he was there that morning. There may have been some indication that the minister would have something to say about him that day—there is now no knowing—but suddenly Mr Wilkie was interrupted from the body of the kirk. There were still no pews in the church. Apart from a few seats for officials of the trade incorporations, and a few chairs belonging to local dignitaries, who paid for that privilege, the men all stood as at an open-air meeting. 'Friend' shouted Hector to the minister, 'I would know by what authority thou doest these things', and he went on 'in severall extravagant expressions to upbraid and scoffe at a high rate' as a later report put it.

After the first shock those standing next to Hector moved in and overpowered him. He was bundled out of the kirk and over the bridge to the tolbooth, where he was shut in. As the Coalhill had not then been built up, there was a clear view between the kirk and the tolbooth, and over the bridge between the two buildings there now developed a great disturbance, for the other Quakers had turned out in force and made a great din. Meanwhile in the church Mr Wilkie tried to proceed with the service as usual. His practice was to follow the sermon with a session of catechising the congregation. Hector Allan however continued shouting abuse from the tolbooth window and the rest of the Quakers kept up their vociferous support for their leader. This was intolerable. Word was sent to the Canongate, and the magistrates had Mr Allan taken to the Canongate tolbooth, which was a more formidable prison than the Leith jail. The case came before the Privy Council the following Thursday, and Hector was sent to the prison on the Bass Rock until the whole matter could be properly investigated.

Towards the end of June the Lords of the Privy Council received a full report on Hector Allan. It appeared that for several years past 'having taken up the profession of a Quaker' Allan had been involved with a number of disorderly meetings both at his own house and elsewhere. Not only in Leith, but also at other ports on the east coast he had taken up the Quaker cause, fulminating against the Kirk and its ministers. He had made trouble at Prestonpans and at Aberdeen, and was a well-known character with a following, certainly in Leith, where, it was suggested, his adherents had put him up to making his protest in the parish kirk. The short, sharp sentence on Allan was a fine of 2000 merks, and he was to remain in prison until the fine was paid. With that, the seaman Quaker of Leith disappears from history.

About this time a new development in the parish was the establishment of a ropework on a site between the Sand port and the Citadel. From the early sixteenth century, when Newhaven was founded by James IV to build a Scots navy, a ropework was said to have existed there. Nothing is known of the work at that period, but in 1638 Patrick Wood got a tack of a site east of Newhaven, where he operated a ropework until his death, after which the site lay empty and derelict until 1663, when King Charles granted a monopoly for ropemaking in Scotland to James Davidson, who sold the monopoly to James Deans, a Canongate bailie. Deans, with his son, tried to make a profit from ropes, but the venture failed, and the monopoly ran out. The ropework at Newhaven was later to be revived by another son of James Deans but in the meantime a Frenchman, Jean Debaut, started his ropework next to the Citadel, intending to make ships' rigging. Being adajacent to the shipyards it was ostensibly a much better site than Newhaven, and the business then started continued quietly until the mid-eighteenth century, when it was known principally as a manufactory of sailcloth.

In the year 1682, when Jean Debaut set up his ropework, a second minister, for some obscure reason, was admitted to North Leith. Thomas Wilkie was still in his prime, and was not translated to the Tron Kirk until 1687, but for his last five years in Leith he had the Rev James Hutcheson assisting him. Hutcheson also was moved from Leith in 1687 and translated to Greyfriars, Edinburgh. That was a year long to be remembered in the Scottish Church, for in June King James made a proclamation to the effect that all his subjects were henceforth to be allowed 'to meet and serve God after their own way, be it in private houses, chapels, or places purposely hired or built for that use'. This was greeted with immense relief, for now Presbyterians and Episcopalians, Roman Catholics and Quakers could worship as they wished. In South Leith there now began a four-year struggle to induce the Episcopalians to quit the parish kirk. North Leith was spared any such wrangle, for with the departure of Thomas Wilkie and James Hutcheson, both Episcopalian, the vacancy was speedily filled by recalling John Knox, who had been deprived of his charge at North Leith twenty-five years previously. He was reinstalled within a month of the King's proclamation; but he was an old man, scarcely fit for an active minstry. He died eight months later. On 5 September 1687 'the haill inhabitants' called James Lundie and, with his ministry North Leith entered upon a new phase of its history.

CHAPTER 3

Presbyterian Life and Worship

Daniel Defoe visited Leith, and published his observations in 1724:

> There are two Churches at Leith, and very large and very full they are, and so indeed are all the Churches in the City, for the People of Scotland do not wander about on the Sabbath-days, as in England; and even those who may have no more Religion than enough, yet Custom has made it almost natural to them, they all go to the Kirk.

Defoe was looking at the first generation of Presbyterians in Scotland—that is, the first generation of those who were free to apply their Presbyterian views and principles as an established national Church. Having survived thirty years of Episcopalian government they were now set on operating the Presbyterian system with no more toleration for other forms than the Episcopalians or Roman Catholics had shown when they had power. Each year the Edinburgh presbytery sent out a questionnaire asking for a return of known Papists in every parish, and in North Leith these were easily counted—the Duke of Gordon and members of his family, living in the Citadel; Francis Gordon and his spouse, Dr Alexander and his son, Mrs Collieson and Mrs Margaret Gall, all in the Duke's household; a certain William Wallace, also in the Citadel, and Anne Gibb, who was a Mrs Smith, living on the Coalhill. There were also the known Episcopalians, with their 'outed' ministers, worshipping under restrictions and closely watched as most of them were Jacobites.

With the establishment of Presbyterianism a fresh drive was made for strict Church discipline. Apart from the few opponents of the Establishment, everyone was expected in Church on Sunday as a normal habit. Church attendance was accepted as a basic religious duty of every man and woman in the community. They were not all fervent, and religious knowledge did not amount to much among the people; but ignorance was all the more reason for going to church, where something might be learned. Most boys and girls attended the parish school for two years, learning to read and write. With that period behind them however, there was small chance of ever practising these skills. Working folk possessed no books—few even had a Bible—and in adult life there was seldom any need for writing beyond an occasional signature. Ministers were well aware of these difficulties, so that normally in the Sunday service the sermon was preceded by a 'lecture', which was a Scripture reading, in which the minister or reader would take a verse or two at a time, explaining the meaning and offering comment. The lecture was a Sunday lesson for the congregation. Catechising was another form of teaching by question and answer. Many ministers wrote their own catechisms and used them for the congregation. Communicant membership of the Church was allowed to those able to repeat the Lord's Prayer, the Ten Commandments and the Apostle's Creed. There were of course always reasons preventing some folk from attending church, and there were always some folk determined not to attend, if that could be managed. To check on non-attenders, both North Leith and Newhaven were searched through each Sunday, both forenoon and afternoon. The important thing in church attendance was to get there in time for the sermon. The searchers, in couples, left the kirk after the lecture and before the sermon, to do their rounds, and reported to the kirk session, which met every Tuesday, when there was also a mid-week service.

In the early years of the Presbyterian establishment, the Tuesday service began at 9 am in winter, and from mid-April this was brought forward to 8 am for the summer months. In 1744 it was decided that the mid-week service would be more conveniently held in the afternoon, so in winter the service was moved to 3 pm, moving to 6 pm for the summer. There was no compulsion to attend the mid-week service as there was for Sunday worship. Changes in arrangements for public worship were always notified to the South Leith kirk session also.

A major development took place in the autumn of 1708, when the kirk session minute for 12 October notes briefly:

> A proposal was made for filling up the body of the church with seats for the conveniency of severalls who want accommodation.

This introduction of fixed pews, no doubt at the desire mainly of the elderly, who found long standing very trying, brought about a marked change in the general atmosphere of divine worship. The long tradition of strolling around in church and gossiping with friends and neighbours while children ran around shouting to each other before the service started, and the scant attention to punctuality, all of which made calling the people to order difficult—this all had to change with the introduction of seats for everyone. Within a few years the change in behaviour in church was remarkable. Defoe, viewing the scene shortly after the pews had been brought in, was impressed:

> They have also one very good Custom as to their Behaviour in the Church, which I wish were practised here, namely, that after the Sermon is over, and the Blessing given, they all look round upon their Friends, and especially to Persons of Distinction, and make their Civilities and Bows as we do here, for, by the Way, the Scots do not want Manners. But if any Person come in

when the Worship is begun, he takes notice of no Body,
nor any Body of him; whereas here we make our Bows
and our Cringes in the Middle of our very Prayers.

The pews introduced a better sense of order and decorum.

The pulpit was set in the middle of one of the long walls of
the kirk, and when pews were brought in they were set to face
the pulpit from all sides. There was no baptismal font or
permanent communion table, but the stool of repentance still
stood as of old at the pillar beside the pulpit. Variously
referred to elsewhere in Scotland as the cutty stool or
creepy stool, in North Leith it was still 'the pillar' or 'the
ordinary place'—a euphemism that is recorded from the early
eighteenth century.

The sacrament of the Lord's Supper was not celebrated at
any particular time. It took place once a year on a Sunday
which was agreed, organised and prepared for over a lengthy
period. In 1709 the minister asked the elders in mid-July to
think of a suitable time for the sacrament, and a fortnight later
it was thought that with so many men from North Leith and
Newhaven away to the herring drave, and with the harvest
expected to follow closely after their return, some time in
September or October would appear to be the earliest date for
the great event. Before raising the matter in the kirk session
the minister had been long at work in preparation for the
sacrament, as he had toured the congregation examining all
those proposing to communicate at the next celebration.

On 23 August it was decided to have the sacrament at the
end of September, when the harvest ought to be over, and the
elders were enjoined 'to a tender and Circumspect Walk, and
to have a Strick ete to any Disorder in their several Quarters'.
But there were more complications. At the communion
service the bread and wine were served to people seated round
a table brought into the church for the occasion. An address
was given, the elements dispensed, and then those round the
table left and their places were taken by others, who in their
turn heard an address and received the elements. These

successive table services made for a very long diet of worship, which continued all day. At the same time crowds of people outside in the churchyard were waiting their turn, and they were addressed by a minister preaching from a little rostrum under a canopy. All this activity required several ministers to take it in turns to relieve each other during the day. It was advisable therefore for North Leith and South Leith to choose separate Sundays for the celebration. On this occasion in 1709 it was found that South Leith had chosen the same Sunday as North Leith for the sacrament. After some talk it was agreed to allow a fortnight to elapse between the two celebrations.

The inordinate length of these services meant that some members did not receive the sacrament at all; they could then attend South Leith or any other church within reasonable distance, on the local sacramental Sunday. But these services attracted crowds who had no intention of communicating. They came to the churchyard and made a social occasion out of it. This is what Robert Burns in Ayrshire, later in the century, knew as the Holy Fair. Edinburgh presbytery was perturbed about this abuse, and in January 1711 the presbytery's Committee on Difficult Cases was asked to propose a remedy. In due course the Rev John Wilson of North Leith received a report and proposal from that committee which he brought before the kirk session:

> They took under consideration how to prevent the great profanation of the Lord's day by the flocking of Multitudes of Idle People to the West Kirk, Cannongate and Leith Churches when the Sacrament of the Lord's Supper is administrate there upon Pretence to hear Sermon in the Church Yeard, whereas many do only vaig about and spend the Lord's day idly, and those who communicate are greatly incommoded by the Throng of Persons who do not communicate, and the said Committee having considered the same, they gave it as their Overture, that there should be no Sermon at such Occasions, but in the Churches, and for the better

Convenience of Communicants, that the said holy
Sacrament should be given in these Churches, all upon the
same Day, as its done in the Churches of Edr, and to make
up the Loss that good People may be at through their not
having the holy Sacrament so frequently administrate to
them who used to attend the same in those Churches, that
the Communion be given in each of those Churches and
also in Edr twice in the year. The Presbytery having
considered the said Report, thought fit before they come
to any Conclusion thereanent, to transmitt the same to the
several Sessions concerned, that they may give their
Opinion about the said Overture to the Presbytery.

The kirk session was happy to agree with the suggestion that
the churchyard preaching should cease, and sermons be
delivered only in church. They were very much against the
proposal that the four neighbouring parishes of Canongate,
the West Kirk (St Cuthbert's), North and South Leith should
all celebrate the sacrament on the same day. The third
proposal, that there should in future be a twice-yearly
sacrament they accepted, albeit reluctantly.

North Leith's objection to celebrating the sacrament in all
four churches on the same day was understandable. The elders
pointed out that the other three churches were collegiate, each
having at least two ministers, who could share the heavy
duties of the sacramental season. Further, it was impossible
for North Leith to decide on any particular Sunday for the
sacrament several weeks in advance. The majority of the male
parishioners were seamen, and many others worked on the
land in various capacities. If the sacramental Sunday were to
be decided simply by the calendar, the weather might make it
unsuitable for many in North Leith.

Far more than Sunday services had to be considered when
the sacrament was to be dispensed. For the people at large the
sacramental season was a week's holiday. This began
on Thursday—a day of 'fasting and humiliation—when a
preparatory service was held. Friday was intended as an

opportunity for private prayer, meditation and Bible reading, but in practice was simply a holiday. On Saturday another preparatory service was held, after which tokens were given out to those asking for them. These communion tokens— small discs, squares, lozenges or some shape of lead or other base metal—were the forerunners of the communion card. They were not distributed by the elders. The minister and kirk session stood in the doorway of the church and handed out tokens as they were asked for. And some were refused if they were known to be guilty of sin for which they had not repented or made amends. Tokens were collected by the elders on duty at the communion table on Sunday before the communicant was allowed to sit down. The long day of services on Sunday was followed on Monday by a thanksgiving service, and on Tuesday by a further service attended by those who had not been present on Monday. As the sacramental season took up so much time it was not practicable to have too frequent celebrations. Working people could not afford many holidays. The Reformers in the sixteenth century had not intended such infrequent celebrations of the Lord's Supper, but the elaborate organization the Kirk had developed around the sacrament made frequent celebrations difficult. Later in the eighteenth century however, a pattern of spring and autumn celebrations became normal.

On the Tuesday evening after the sacrament five of the elders were detailed to meet with the treasurer and distribute the money collected at the various services of the past week to the poor of the parish. At the same time an honorarium was given to the beadle and other paid servants of the church, in consideration of the extra work they had had over the sacramental season.

In October 1717 a committee of the presbytery visited North Leith to examine the kirk session records. They were satisfied with the way the minutes were kept, but pointed out two irregularities. None of the elders had ever signed the Confession of Faith, and there appeared to be no deacons.

These two matters must be put right at once 'according to the Word of God and Constitutione of this Church'. There had been deacons formerly, before the imposition of Episcopalian government, but none had been appointed since the turn-round to Presbyterianism again. This omission was now remedied, and deacons appointed to take responsibility for the well-being of the poor of the parish. A few years later, in January 1724, new elders and deacons were appointed. There is no mention of ordination: office-bearers were appointed to serve for three years. A committee of the session was asked to make recommendations and they reported in February:

1 The Session should actually consist of the number of fifteen Elders, whereof at least there should be nine who for ordinary have their fixed abode at home, and nine Deacons.
2 That a particular Quarter and Bounds be appointed for each Elder and Deacon, which they are strictly to notice.
3 That there be a new Election of Session at the end of every third Year.
4 That upon the Decrease or Removal of any Elder and Deacon out of the Parish, another be chosen in his room with all convenient Speed.

The stipulation in the first proposal that nine of the fifteen elders should 'for ordinary have their fixed abode at home' has regard to the fact that many of the men in the parish were seamen. Some of these might be suitable for the eldership, but being at sea for lengthy periods they would not be regular attenders at session meetings, or available for district or other duties except when ashore. Absence from or late arrival at session meetings without reasonable excuse entailed a fine, which went to the poor box. The quarters, or elders' districts, were defined by this same committee in June 1724:

1 From the east end of the Parish to the Bridge End, comprehending the whole Coallhill.

2 From the Bridge End to the walk dike, Comprehending the back of the Church.

3 The whole North side of the Street, from the whin staks to the sand port.

4 From the sand port to the Kirkland on the south, inclusive.

5 From the Kirkland on the south inclusive, to the foot of the broad wynd on the wet side.

6 From the foot of the broad wynd inclusive on the west to the Bridge End.

7 Cittadel, links and Damhead.

New Haven

8 From the Crew Inclusive all the south side of the Street and part of the north side of the Street of New Haven, that surrounds the old Glass-house.

9 From the Bounds of the old Glass-house to the West End of the Toun on the North Side of the Street of New Haven.

NB: That the Elders and Deacons Inspect Especially their own Bounds, to prevent disorders, especially on the Lord's day, as also that they enquire for Testimonials from Strangers, and Consider the case of the poor and sick, and if they shall find disorders in any other Quarter of the town, that they join with the Elders of that Quarter in order to remove them.

From the fifth and sixth quarters described above, it will be seen that there was a Broad Wynd in North Leith which was, of course, quite distinct from the Broad Wynd in South Leith running between the Shore and Water Street. The elders and deacons took responsibility for policing the village and maintaining public order. The directive to 'enquire for Testimonials from Strangers' was important. At that period no one could leave the parish where he belonged to live and work elsewhere without a certificate of good character. Lacking this he would not easily find employment in a strange place. The elders of the parish received these certificates and informed the kirk session.

Church door collections all went into the poor box. The poor were destitute. If, from illness, disability or old age, a man was unemployed, no government or public money was available to him. There were far more poor than could ever be adequately relieved from the poor box. Every winter there were deaths from starvation, and in a bad winter, especially after a poor harvest, that number greatly increased. Fees for every kind of service went to the poor, and at a baptism in the kirk there was a charge for behoof of the poor. Baptisms more frequently took place at the manse or at home however, and the poor box suffered. Realising this, the kirk session in January 1724 made the appropriate move:

> The Session considering how much the Collections are Impaired by the frequency of Baptizing Children in the house, they Resolved Unanimously that any person who shall desire that benefit hereafter, shall pay to the Treasurer one pound Scots toties quoties.

And if one pound seems substantial, it should be remembered that one pound Scots was then valued at one-twelfth of its English equivalent. None the less 1/8d sterling was a sizeable fee in Scotland.

At the end of August 1724 the minister, John Wilson, died, and in the ensuing quest for a new minister four heritors claimed the right to vote in the election as landowners in the parish. Now in North Leith the heritors *qua* heritors, had no right to vote. The right to call a minister lay exclusively in the hands of the kirk session and all the inhabitants. James Law of Hillhousefield was the only one of the four inheritors claiming to vote, who was actually living in his own house in the parish. Thomas Broun of Bonnytoun lived in South Leith parish, but three acres of his land lay in North Leith adajacent to the Hillhousefield estate. Laurence Findlayson was an elder in South Leith parish kirk and was one of the three Masters of the King James Hospital. The hospital was proprietor of six acres of land in North Leith, so Mr Findlayson represented that interest. Another South Leith elder, Bailie Gilbert Mathieson, represented South Leith kirk session, who were proprietors of land at Newhaven, where they conducted a head court every year. In view of these various interests the four claims to vote in the North Leith election were allowed.

Mr George Lindsay was inducted to the charge of North Leith in the spring of 1725 and very soon discovered that, while the parish was rural in its aspect, there was no lack of social problems. The parish school had originally met in a house belonging to George Rankin, a local stone-mason. The yard attached to the house made it convenient as a playground for the scholars. The kirk session rented these premises, but in 1698 they were able to buy the building from Mr Rankin for 1000 merks. This satisfactory arrangement was disturbed when in 1722 a petition was presented to the kirk session from Dougal McPherson, who proposed to erect a school on the Coalhill, where he would teach English. This presented a problem. Legally no school could be set up in the parish without a licence from the kirk session, and the elders were strongly of opinion that a school on Coalhill would take scholars away from the parish school. McPherson, however, was an ex-serviceman. He had been a sergeant in the army, and was now a Chelsea Pensioner—an outpensioner. He must therefore have had a long and meritorious record in the army. Now for men with such a record King Charles II had introduced a system of 'king's freemen'. A king's freeman was not paid any pension, but he had the right to practise any trade or skill he might possess without the obligation to join a trade incorporation with the expensive entry fees and quarterly contributions. Dougal McPherson stood in that category. Also, since the Union of the Parliaments in 1707, there had been a rising demand for the teaching of English, so Mr McPherson would not lack pupils. Considering all this, the session nevertheless forbad the erection of the school, but three years later, in 1725, with Mr Lindsay as moderator, the session learned that not only had McPherson built his school, but was teaching English reading, writing and arithmetic. The elders were powerless to do anything about it.

Two years later there was a different response to an application to open a school in the parish. Hitherto the parish school appears to have catered for boys only, perhaps owing to the lack of accommodation for girls. In May 1727 Anne Inglis, the widow of Robert Taylor, a merchant in Queensferry, sought permission to open a school for teaching girls to read and sew. She was interviewed, declared she was well satisfied with the government of Church and State, that she had and owned the Confession of Faith, and the Assembly's Catechism, that she attended Church and would enjoin her scholars to do the same. She got her licence, and it may be noted that she applied and obtained permission to open her school under 'her own name', as the Scots have it. The fact that she had been Mrs Taylor did not deprive her of her right to her maiden name. Presumably she had had no children.

There was no escaping the burden of the poor. At the end of the seventeenth century the poor were defined as those destitute folk who had been born in the parish, or had been resident there for at least seven years; but in 1731, when the kirk session compiled a new poor roll, the minimum residence in the parish was reduced to three years. The situation was always confused by vagrants and sturdy beggars who did not belong to Leith but made themselves a nuisance about the place. Strenuous efforts were made to get rid of these sorners, who often demanded money or food with menaces, but, Leith being a port, they remained a problem. Genuine local beggars were given badges for identification, and were free to beg within the parish.

The support of foundlings was a charge of the kirk session. In such a poverty-stricken community it was not unknown for newly-born babies to be abandoned. A girl giving birth to a child in abject poverty, with no prospect of being able to maintain the baby, might leave it exposed, knowing that the local kirk session would look after it when found. In a village, however, this kind of thing could not easily happen without the mother being known, so she would contrive to leave it elsewhere. In April 1737 a child was found exposed in Newhaven. The kirk session argued that since Newhaven had always insisted on looking after its own poor, and renewed this insistence at the entry of each successive minister to the parish, the foundling ought to be the responsibility of the Free Fishermen. The Fishermen maintained that the child did not belong to any Newhaven woman, and they wanted nothing to do with it. Mr Lindsay the minister proposed a compromise which was accepted, whereby the session would pay for all the child's clothes, and the Fishermen would pay half the maintenance costs. So the baby was given to a wet nurse, and would remain a charge on the kirk session until old enough to earn its own living.

Education, even at the parish school, was not free. The fees amounted to no more than a few pence weekly, but poor folk could not pay any fees. If they thought any of their children bright enough to benefit from schooling they could apply to the session who in the mid-eighteenth century were supporting a dozen children at school, paying for all of them. Sometimes a well-disposed elder, or the neighbour of a poor family, would offer to pay for a bright boy's schooling, with the hearty approval of the session.

At the best of times there was barely enough money available to provide for all those on the poor roll. When food was scarce and dear even the better-off people had less to spare for the poor, so that the greater the need the less were the resources from which that need might be met. From time to time appeals were made to the heritors, but the situation was sometimes desperate. The winter of 1740–1 was a time of famine. Riots broke out and mobs attacked granaries for the meal in store they could not afford to buy. In May 1740, well before that year's disastrous harvest, the kirk session were so concerned at the steep rise in the number of poor in the parish that they decided to restrict the list to those confined to bed by sickness, or who were aged and infirm. The able-bodied would be given badges and told to fend for themselves. When the harvest of that year failed, the grim winter that followed claimed many lives, and in May 1741, with the whole nation hoping and praying for a better harvest, the General Assembly recommended:

> a ffast for the distressed State of the Land by the Scarcity ond Famine wee are groaning under, the dangerous and Expensive War wee are engaged in (with Spain) to be observed on Thursday the Eighteenth June.

This was intimated from the pulpit in North Leith:

> and all seriously Exhorted to a due observation thereof, for averting the Judgements hanging over our Heads, and heavier Strokes yet to be Inflicted on Account of our Many Sins and grievous Backslidings.

To the intense relief of everyone the harvest of 1741 was abundant, and the Presbytery of Edinburgh at the end of September issued an Act:

> setting apart Thursday the fifteenth of October for solemn Prayer and Thanksgiving for the good and plentiful Harvest and Crowning the Year with his goodness . . .

But the problem of the poor continued to escalate. On 14 January 1757 the elders heard from Mr Lindsay that a group of Edinburgh merchants had clubbed together to purchase a cargo of oatmeal which was now stored in a cellar on Sheriff Brae. It was intended to sell this at a reduced rate of tenpence ha'penny per peck to poor families in South and North Leith. The Provost of Edinburgh had sent Mr Lindsay a number of tickets, each to be exchanged for a peck of meal.

The Session after hearing said Representation were glad that it had entred into the hearts of Gentlemen of Substance thus to pity and relieve the poor, and agreed that the Tickets sent here be given to the Elders and Deacons, to be distribute to such as are needy and apply for them, which was done accordingly.

At that same meeting Mr Lindsay also announced that he had received from Mr George Chalmers a donation of £5.00 sterling, which was to be distributed without delay to the most needy people in the parish. Three months later the kirk session received information of the irregular marriage of George Chalmers with Elizabeth Stephen. There was probably a connection between those incidents. Irregular or clandestine marriage remained a problem in North Leith, as in South Leith, for many a long day. The trouble was not exclusive to Leith, but the great majority of irregular marriages in Scotland happened in Leith and Edinburgh. An irregular marriage was one which took place without reference to the parish minster. No written record of such a union was kept, so that it was difficult and often impossible to prove it.

The problem was compounded by the fact that irregular marriage was legal. In Scots law, if a couple declared before at least two witnesses that they took each other for husband and wife, that declaration constituted a legal, valid marriage. However, if a girl contracted an irregular marriage with a man in the armed forces, she would not be officially informed of his death. She would then be unable to show that she was a widow, perhaps with children, and would receive no help from the kirk session. A clandestine marriage might be kept secret, but when the girl gave birth to her first child and sought baptism for it, the whole story had to be confessed to the kirk session. The minister then rebuked the couple, exhorted them to live together as Christians, and fined them. They then had to pay the normal fee for a regular marriage, then meet the usual charge for a baptism—altogether a more expensive business than a regular marriage and baptism would have been, although young couples who were plainly poverty-stricken were often dealt with leniently.

By no means all of these were furtive affairs between silly lassies and scoundrels. Many respectable, bein folk were married irregularly. In former times and in remoter parts, not served by priest or minister, various forms of irregular marriage, such as 'handfasting', were practised. These conditions never applied to Leith, but in the seventeenth century one consequence of the continued intransigence between different denominations in the Church was a rapid rise in the number of clandestine marriages. Presbyterian ministers 'outed' when episcopal government was imposed in 1662 could no longer conduct 'regular' marriage, but many in their former congregations sympathised with them and went to them for irregular marriage. After 1689 the same thing happened with the 'outed' episcopal ministers, who conducted irregular marriage for their former adherents. But the re-introduction of patronage in 1712 soon drove the number of clandestine marriages to epidemic proportions. Patronage was the system whereby in a vacancy a minister could be presented to the charge by the patron—generally the largest landowner in the parish—without reference to the wishes of the congregation. This did not affect North Leith, where the people themselves were the patrons, but it caused widespread resentment, and was the principal cause of the formation of the Secession Kirk in 1733. In Leith a secession congregation formed after a disputed settlement in South Leith in 1740. Adherents of the secession from both South and North Leith then took to worshipping separately, and eventually, as an Antiburgher congregation, called their own minister. All marriages in the Secession Kirk were irregular.

In this unstable situation a number of men were known to be conducting irregular marriages on a scale that indicated this was their livelihood. Ministers deprived of their charges for various reasons were hard put to it to make an income, and were only too willing to unite a young couple in holy matrimony for a suitable fee, with no questions asked and no record made. David Strang conducted many such marriages in Leith and Edinburgh, and on 28 June 1737 the kirk session of North Leith heard from Michael Robertson and Margaret Campbel that they had been irregularly married by the said Mr Strang:

> ... Mr David Strang, a Person lying under the Sentence of the Greater Excommunication, which was publickly Intimate to all the Churches of the Presbytery of Edinburgh, and proper Admonitions given, at least by our Minister here, for all Persons to shun unnecessary Converse with the said Mr Strang, YET NOTWITHSTANDING not a few continue still such Illegal Contempt of the Laws of the Nation both Civil and Ecclesiastick, THE SESSION THEREFORE find it absolutely necessary on their part to Endeavour to put a Stop to such irregularities by Censuring such Delinquents in a more publick Manner than by a Sessional Rebuke to the terror of others, And appoint the said Parties Michael Robertson and Margaret Campbel to be rebuked before the Congregation Sabbath nixt after divine worship forenoon the third of July ensuing, and refers them to the Civil Magistrate for the Crime of Adultery or Bigamy.

David Strang had been minister of Cabrach, near Huntly, but was deposed for neglecting his duty. He came to Edinburgh, where he became much in favour as a celebrator of clandestine unions. For his persistence in these activities he was excommunicated. As this made no difference to him he was arrested, imprisoned and sentenced to banishment. Somehow he managed to avoid this and continued, even in prison, to celebrate irregular marriages until 1744, when he died in prison at the age of seventy.

Strang's death did nothing to lessen the number of irregular marriages. In the next twelve years William Jameson and David Paterson each performed well over a hundred such unions. In January 1754 Aeneas McKinnon and Jean Smith confessed to the session that they had been irregularly married by David Paterson. The session had previously accepted other couples married by the same Mr Paterson, but this time they made a stand and refused to acknowledge the marriage as legal. They had no right to do this but were clearly exasperated, so the couple 'were upon a remorse regularly proclaimed and married this day before the session, after being rebuked for their former irregularity'. But that, it is worth noting, was the only regular marriage performed in North Leith during that whole year.

The Church never solved the problem of irregular marriage—a practice rife in England also, where the notorious Fleet marriages were a public scandal. Two acts were published in 1753 and 1781, covering 'England, Wales and Berwick', providing that marriages celebrated in churches other than parish churches, and by ministers other than parish ministers, should be deemed regular; and in 1784 these provisions were extended to Scotland. This had an immediate effect. There was no longer any inducement to resort to ministers of doubtful standing and character; any minister in any church of any Christian denomination could now perform a regular marriage. The number of irregular unions fell off dramatically.

George Lindsay, ordained to North Leith in April 1725, served for almost forty years in what remained essentially a rural charge, although closely linked with both South Leith and Canongate. The year after his settlement Mr Lindsay married, and three years later asked the kirk session if they would allow him to rent the steeple room as part of the manse. The reason for this odd request was not recorded. The steeple room, over the church, had served originally as a session room, but was now rented to a tailor for a dwelling. Mr Lindsay said he was perfectly satisfied with the manse, which was adjacent to the church, but that he would like the use of the steeple room, which would be an extension to his kitchen if the separating wall were to be provided with a door. He was prepared to pay for the alteration, pay rent for the extra accommodation, and would restore the stone and lime wall again if he gave up the use of the room. The session agreed, and charged rent of three pounds Scots for the room. Yet six years later a report on the steeple house, as it was called, said that it had last been occupied by a shipmaster, and stood in need of urgent repair. So Mr Lindsay's occupancy had not lasted long, and his reason for using it at all remains a mystery.

The need to repair the steeple house in 1735 however, was but a small matter coming at the end of a summer of great anxiety for the congregation. At the beginning of June Captain Alex Johnston, shipmaster, and treasurer to the session, with Patrick Robertson, shipbuilder, and also an elder, had suspected for some time that all was not well with the church roof. They examined it and found it extensively affected by dry rot. They called in two wrights from Edinburgh known to be experienced in such matters, and they confirmed the elders' suspicions. The roof was in a hazardous state and ought to be pulled down at once. Before reporting to the session they called in William Adam, the famous architect, and father of the even more famous brothers John, James and Robert. William agreed that the roof was dangerous and ought to be replaced by a roof of different design.

After further examination the session agreed there was no alternative. Mr Adam was commissioned to design a new roof, and the elders went on to consider how they might raise the very large sum of money that would be needed. It was borne in on them then that North Leith's proud record of having built and maintained their own kirk hitherto, had its disadvantages. In other places the heritors would have been responsible for repairing the kirk, but in North Leith they had no such obligation. All that could be expected from the heritors would be any contribution they cared to make as parishioners. It was decided that the various bodies owning pews should share the burden of paying for the roof. This meant that the kirk session would divide the expense with the trade incorporations having galleries or lofts. In particular, with the new style of roof, some of the pillars in the church would be removed, and both the Carpenters' and Cordiners'

(Shoemakers) galleries would require to be rebuilt. The result would be more commodious accommodation, and these corporations agreed to pay for the alterations in their part of the church. A collection was organised to cover the whole parish, and finally a 'Humble Petition and Address' was presented to the Lord Provost, Bailies and Town Council of Edinburgh, and to the presbytery for permission to take up a collection throughout the city and suburbs in aid of this good cause. William Adam's estimate for the whole work amounted to £363 sterling, which was a very large sum.

The work was successfully completed, and paid for with a struggle.

> The Session considering the many obligations the Parish in general and particularly the Session ly under to Patrick Robertson, ship builder, one of their Members, and Chief Manager in the late Reparation of the Church, who first happily discovered the Failure of the Roof, procured the Scheme of the new Roof drawn by Mr William Adam, Architect, According to which the said Mr Robertson has with much Fatigue, great Pains and Exact diligence seen the Work now done and finished to perfection and the Satisfaction of all concerned, for which the Session return him their hearty thanks.

The minute goes on to say that, had the session been able to afford it, the least they could have offered him in the way of acknowledgement of the debt they owed him, would be a free seat in the church for him and his descendants. Unfortunately, in their present straitened circumstances after the expense of re-roofing the church, they felt unable to do this. However, seat rents were now to be increased, but Mr Robertson would continue to possess his pew at the old rent of £9.00 Scots yearly. And this indeed would be a bargain, as his pew would now be enlarged by the removal of a stone pillar which hitherto had blocked the pulpit from view.

Church attendance was still more or less compulsory, but

the behaviour of children in church was a continuing problem. It has been seen that as far back as 1616 David Forrester the minister had to intimate that squalling infants must not be brought to church. A hundred and thirty years later older children were posing a problem. In February 1745:

> It was represented by Several of the Members that many people in the Lofts and likewise below were much disturbed in time of Worship, by the Noise of Idle Boys; for the preventing of which in time coming the Session appoints the Baillie officer to sit att the foot of Lady Bruce's seat, and to take particular Notice of such Boys as they find disturbing the Hearers, and to put them out of the Church.

That was the year of the Forty-five Rebellion, when in September the Highland Host under Prince Charles Edward Stewart occupied Edinburgh, bringing church services to an end for some weeks. The rebels got no welcome from the Edinburgh presbytery. For a while church life was suspended, and when North Leith kirk session convened again on 19 November:

> The Moderator did Intimate from the Pulpit the first Sabbath of September last with suitable Exhortations, An Act of the Presbytrie of Edinburgh of date the twenty-ninth day of August last for a ffast to be observed within their bounds on Thursday the fifth of the said Month of Septr, on accound of the dangerous and expensive War we are engaged in with powerful United Enemies, and how much a Holy Just and Righteous God has been of late testifying his displeasure against us by their rapid success abroad, and by suffering a Popish and Malignant Party, with the Pretender's Son at their head, to disturb the peace of our Native Country, by a wicked and Rebellious Insurrection att home &c. which day was religiously observed by this Congregation, there being Sermon fore

and afternoon by our own Minr from the 6th verse& of
the eighth chapter of Esther 'for how can I endure to see
the evil that shall come unto my People, Or how can I
endure to see the destruction of my Kindred?'

That was the only recorded comment made by the kirk session
on the very unwelcome intrusion on the city by the Jacobite
army.

In the 1750s there was a fresh outbreak of dry rot, and some
of the seating was replaced. A skylight over the Hillhousefield
seat was so rotten that rain was coming in. The session
ordered the skylight to be shut up 'as the Church has light
enough without it'.

About this time Mr Lindsay's health began to fail. He had
trouble with his chest, and complained to the session that his
room was very smoky and harmful to him in winter. He
suggested that if the session would 'height the Lumheid to see
and prevent the Smoak' he himself would bear half the
expense. This was agreed but the minister's health did not
improve. It was soon obvious that Mr Lindsay could no
longer cope with all the work of the ministry so, in 1756, Mr
Spears, a probationer, was engaged as assistant. The arrangement was that the minister would provide his assistant with
bed, board and washing, and the kirk session would pay him
£10 per annum, and a further £10 would be made up from
voluntary subscriptions throughout the parish. This satisfied
all parties, but Mr Spears, after little more than a year, was
settled in a charge of his own, and another probationer,
William Porteous, was engaged on the same terms. The
following year, 1759, Mr Lindsay announced his intention of
dispensing the sacrament early in June, as he intended 'to go
for his health to the Goat whey a few weeks in the Summer
time'. It was not recorded whether the goat whey was in any
way beneficial, but Mr Lindsay, a few months later, was
involved with the greatest project of his ministry.

The opening of the Edinburgh Charity Workhouse at
Bristo in 1753 was an event of great importance to the large

floating population of vagrants. The possibility of receiving free board and lodging was enough to attract beggars from far and near. In addition to the local poor Leith had always been pestered with 'foreign' vagrants and this problem worsened after the Edinburgh workhouse opened. The Bailies of Leith issued repeated warnings to the inhabitants not to receive any beggars except the locals with begging badges. A poorhouse for the local poor was an attractive idea. The streets would be cleared of this nuisance, and outsiders, or 'outrels' as they were called, kept away. South Leith had already examined the idea, but abandoned it for lack of money. In North Leith there was a smiddy with a piece of waste land attached. That building, now tenanted, might be enlarged and converted to make a poorhouse. When the elders approached James Greig the blacksmith, however, he said he was proposing to feu the smiddy ground and extend the building to provide himself with a house. The elders, perforce, had to withdraw.

That was in January 1760. Mr Lindsay was now enthusiastic over the idea of a poorhouse, and brought the matter up again in April. He urged the elders to continue making inquiries for some suitable property 'that they might be free of the great Number of begging Poor that are every day strolling about'. He himself, with John Sime the shipbuilder, a member of session, made contact with William Miller, a seed merchant in the Canongate, who owned property in the Citadel. One house in particular they thought might suit their purpose very well. They discussed their idea with Mr Miller, who became interested and gave them a long lease of a group of houses he owned, approving of the conversion to a poorhouse, and charging a rent of five guineas per annum. Plans and estimates took time, and every penny had to be watched. In March 1762, with the plans approved, it was decided that building materials should be bought as and when bargain lots might be obtainable—a sensible move with several shipbuilders in the congregation. Collecting these materials took up another year, and in the spring of 1763 a start was made on a site just west of the entrance to the Citadel. William Walker, a wright in the Citadel, was engaged as contractor for the whole scheme. He put the work in hand at once, and in August the building was complete, and a committee of the session visited and inspected it.

This was a triumph for George Lindsay who, despite failing health, had persisted with this venture for three years. It was all the more remarkable that a village should have acquired such a social asset, when the populous parish of South Leith, on the other side of the river, had failed in its attempt. William Maitland in 1753, published figures showing North Leith still to be a village:

The Parish of North Leith consists of 6 Divisions

1	Coalhill	80	families	261	Examinable Persons.	
2	Bridge-end & Back of Church	57	"	174	"	"
3	North side of North Leith	69	"	175	"	"
4	South side of North Leith	155	"	427	"	"
5	Citadel, Damhead & Links	47	"	145	"	"
6	Newhaven	98	"	314	"	"
		506		1496		

George Lindsay died just a year after the poorhouse was completed. The parish he had served since 1725 had scarcely changed throughout his ministry. The small area around the church was busy and well-populated, but the remainder of the parish was open country, except for the hamlets of Hillhousefield, Damhead and the little fishing port of Newhaven at the west end. To the city dwellers in the heart of Old Edinburgh, North Leith was an attractive seaside resort with its sparkling river, gently shelving beaches and rolling links. That would all change, but not just yet. There was still a vast difference between the city and the port.

CHAPTER 4

The Reign of Dr Johnston

The parish of North Leith now enjoyed the great benefit of a phenomenally long ministry. That in itself might have been no great blessing, but David Johnston was no ordinary cleric. He was a devoted minister exercising a pronounced gift of leadership. His preaching was never remarkable, but his personality was unforgettable. For fifty-nine years he held the charge of North Leith, and was respected and revered not only in the industrialised end of the parish around the docks and harbour but also in the exclusive fishing village of Newhaven. He came to a thinly populated parish and stayed as it grew and developed into a thriving town. He came to shepherd less than 1500 souls, and by the first official census in 1801 this had grown to over 3200. Ten years later the figure was 4875 'exclusive of men in the Army or Local Militia, Royal Navy, or belonging to Registered Vessels'. By 1821 there were 7025 inhabitants of North Leith, exclusive of the above-mentioned categories. The young thirty-year-old David Johnston was called to what was largely a rural parish; the ninety-year-old Dr Johnston had spiritual oversight of a community five times as great.

This immense increase in the course of little more than half a century, after generations of near stagnation, inevitably brought many strains and produced problems unforeseen in earlier times. Housing the hundreds of incomers, caring for the soaring number of the poor, maintaining even a semblance of the Church discipline of former days, keeping public order and safety with so many strangers infiltrating the settled, traditional life of the older community were all challenges confronting the minister and kirk session of the parish. The village of the 1760s had no sanitation or piped water. There was no street lighting and no one responsible for clearing the dung-heaps blocking the wynds and alleys. Indeed there were no made roads at all, for the Turnpike Road Act of 1763 had not yet affected North Leith. Tolls and toll-houses were still in the future and foot passengers and traffic of all kinds had to make do with tracks broken by pot-holes filled with mud and water in winter and raising clouds of dust in summer. All these areas of public life were radically changed in the course of the two generations of David Johnston's ministry. Inflation also had to be endured and, as people struggled to adjust to the new life-style being thrust on them, the older folk, as always, regretted the passing of the good old days and looked rather sourly on their children's and grandchildren's zest for change.

David Johnston was admitted to the charge on 31 July 1765. The word 'induction' had not yet come into use in connection with the settlement of a minister, so Mr Johnston was 'admitted' after a year-long vacancy. The elders, deacons and inhabitants had agreed to present a call to Mr Johnston, then minister of Langton in Dumfriesshire, in October 1764, but the presbytery delayed granting moderation in the call because of an objection by the Crown, which claimed the right of patronage in North Leith, and the Crown Agent laid before the presbytery a presentation to North Leith in favour of a Mr Philip Morison, together with Mr Morison's letter of acceptance.

The Crown's case was that the King was patron of the Parish of Holyroodhouse, and that when the parish of North Leith had been erected out of that parish the right of patronage was not included, and indeed no change in the patronage was made until the coming of episcopacy, and the erection of the bishopric of Edinburgh, when the patronage of North Leith and many other parishes was given to the

Bishop. When Episcopacy was succeeded by Presbyterianism as the established religion in Scotland, the patronage reverted to the Crown. If North Leith wished to deny this and claim the patronage of their parish, they would have to exhibit their titles to presbytery. The North Leith elders were only too happy to do this, and produced a series of documents beginning with a copy of the Act of 1606 clearly granting the patronage of the parish to 'the haill inhabitants'. They also showed how successive ministers were presented to the charge by 'the haill inhabitants', with the consent of the Bishop during the episcopal ascendancy. When Presbyterianism was established the patronage remained with 'the haill inhabitants' as before. The claim to the patronage advanced by the Crown had no substance, and it is not possible now to understand why it was made; but the presbytery could not ignore it, and the legal arguments and counter claims occupied much time, as the presbytery would only consider consider the matter at its ordinary monthly meetings. In this way the winter of 1764–5 passed while North Leith remained vacant.

One of the first significant happenings following Mr Johnston's settlement was the death of Robert Buchan the session clerk, which happened in January 1766. The session clerk was then a paid employee of the kirk session. He was not an elder, and had no vote in the session. His pay was very small, but he combined the clerkship with the position of parish schoolmaster and lived in the schoolhouse. He was also responsible for congregational singing, and either acted as precentor himself, or provided someone able for the job. The importance or otherwise of the clerkship lay with the man himself. An efficient and conscientious session clerk could wield much influence in the parish and be widely respected, but many clerks were far from ideal. In just a fortnight after Mr Buchan's death his successor was appointed. 'Mr James Gladstones, Preacher of the Gospel, and late Schoolmaster at Biggar, was chosen by a great majority'. This man was an elder brother of one of the North Leith elders, Thomas Gladstones, who had been one of the parish representatives to presbytery during the vacancy. Thomas Gladstones was a corn merchant in Leith, a man of thirty-four, two years older than the minister. Before long David Johnston and Thomas Gladstones were close friends and this friendship continued throughout their lives. Gladstones was to become the grandfather of William Ewart Gladstone, the Victorian statesman and Prime Minister, and he ran his corn merchant's business from a little house on the Coalhill, where one room served as an office. He had come to Leith from Biggar, where his father, a miller and farmer, was a respected elder of the kirk. There was a large family of five sons and six daughters and, after the father's death in 1757, Thomas though the second youngest of the sons, was regarded as the business man of the family. James, his elder brother, had always been intended for the ministry, and in due course he had qualified and been licensed to preach. He did not find a parish, however, and became in common parlance a 'stickit minister'. There were always such men who, well-educated as they were, frequently ended up as 'dominies'—village schoolmasters. James Gladstones had become schoolmaster of Biggar, and it was from there, no doubt through his brother's influence, that he came to Leith. Little more is known about James beyond the fact that he was 'a notorious gossip'.

Shortly after the new session clerk was installed the kirk session was presented with a 'Memorial' from the minister. This long-winded document was simply a request for an increase in stipend. In those days there was no central organization dealing with this matter and the courts of the Church gave no lead to kirk sessions. Normally the heritors were responsible for stipend, and in many parishes where heritors were reluctant to burden themselves with any increase the minister had to raise an action for augmentation of stipend in the Court of Session. In North Leith, where the 'haill inhabitants' were responsible, the request had to be made to the kirk session. David Johnston was clearly embarrassed. He approached the matter cautiously:

Your Memorialist Entertains the highest regard and affection for all his People, and the highest Esteem for his session in particular, and it would give him the deepest concern, if any thing should ever arise that would breed Coldness or Dissension betwixt them.

But he goes on to remind the session of facts with which we in the twentieth century are all too familiar:

The Expence of Living has increased greatly of late, (which they themselves must have felt) owing to the price of Provisions of all kinds being raised almost double to what they were Thirty or Forty Years ago. Your Memorialist has had near Twelve Months Experience how things will answer in the way of Family Expence, when he finds it will be difficult for him to Subsist on the present Stipend, the difference betuixt Living in the Town and Country being very Considerable.

The stipend was paid from a variety of sources—the fish tithes of Leith and Newhaven, the corn tithes of Hillhousefield, the stock and teind of four and a half acres of land, seat rents, and a number of house rents. Income from these funds had risen to almost a hundred pounds over the past seventy years, during which there had been no increase in stipend. As these moneys were expressly intended for stipend, this application for an increase was surely reasonable.

But whatever right in Law or in Equity Your Memorialist may have to an augmentation, he is resolv'd, that unless it be given Voluntarily, he will never Enter into any Process, preferring harmony and peace before any Temporal Interest whatever. But if they shall think it reasonable, and will give him an addition of four hundred merks, Your Memorialist will be pretty much on an Equality with his Brethren in point of income, tho he has almost as much duty to perform as any Two Ministers in the Presbytery in the way of Preaching.

The session replied to this a month later, pointing out that the various funds listed by the minister had to cover not only his stipend, but also the schoolmaster's salary, fees to the session clerk and other lesser payments. In fact there was at present a balance of just £36.2.3 but 'none of the Extraordinaries that affect these funds are charged, as they cannot easily be ascertained'. The session agreed that an increase in stipend was justified, and granted an addition of 300 merks:

> This to commence from Martinmass last and to continue all the days of his life, or his being Minister of this Parish, but it is hereby expressly provided that it shall not extend to his successors in Office, or be considered as part of Legal Stipend, unless the session shall be pleased to renew it by a New Grant.

And so this embarrassing matter was settled for the time being, and it was not raised again until towards the end of the century, when war sent the cost of living soaring once again.

With the advent of the new schoolmaster the session was made aware of the deficiencies of the school and schoolhouse. These buildings were probably thatched cottages from the previous century, now no longer wind and watertight, and too far decayed to be repaired properly. Anything less desperate than these conditions would have found the elders resistant to the development now embarked upon. This was no less than a new school and schoolhouse. The money came from the sale of a house in the Citadel belonging to the session, added to money from the late Captain Johnston, who had left property in the Citadel to be sold for the benefit of the poor. This fortunate concatenation of circumstances made the enterprise so smooth that when the main work was completed in January 1768 the session decided to put in a plaster ceiling, to strengthen the roofing in the garret floor, and to have tirlasses (lattices) made for the lower half of the windows, over and above what had been estimated for. Just then, with the various accounts coming in for the new building, Mr Paterson the treasurer handed in his resignation. His sight was rapidly failing, he was feeling his age and was unable to cope with all the work involved. The session thanked him heartily for his past services, and with no pause at all unanimously voted for Thomas Gladstones to take over as treasurer. So the affairs of the congregation were now administered from day to day by the minister, with the two brothers Gladstones—a close-knit team who were also close friends.

A few months later a row blew up which might easily have ended in costly litigation, but the young minister showed himself to be level-headed and something of a diplomat. A certain John Campbell had begun building a house for himself on land which encroached upon the minister's glebe. Several of the elders had noticed the encroachment as the ground was cleared and the building proceeded. There seems to have been some vagueness in the public mind as to where the precise boundary of the glebe ran, and no one had felt enough assurance to raise the matter.

It was in the early years of the eighteenth century that the land around Edinburgh and Leith was first enclosed. Fields bounded by dykes and hedges were marked out for the first time, and as it took some years to build dykes and plant hedges, march stones were at first employed. Many arguments arose over the exact placing of these stones, and charges were brought against those alleged to have moved them. A Burlaw Court was set up in Leith to hear these allegations and settle arguments. In summer this court met in the open on the Beir Hill—the slope now bounded by Restalrig Road and Lochend Road—but by the mid-century bounds had become largely agreed, and the Burlaw Court had gradually lapsed. At an earlier period the alleged encroachment on the North Leith glebe would have been a case for the Burlaw Court. In September 1768 Mr Johnston informed the session that he had noticed the encroachment, had heard the opinion of several elders, and had approached the presbytery to send a committee to visit the glebe, ascertain the bounds, and speak to Mr Campbell. When challenged, Campbell denied the encroachment, maintaining that he had kept within the ground for which he had a charter. After talking it over with the presbytery committee and Mr Johnston, Campbell said he was willing to feu the whole field where the alleged encroachment had taken place. The minister agreed to this, provided the presbytery and kirk session consented. The proposal was put to the presbytery, who appointed a committee to see Mr Campbell and seal the bargain; but when they met Campbell again they found he had changed his mind, and now wished to buy the field, offering £100 sterling for it. Mr Johnston then employed a 'Land Measurer' to determine the exact size of the field, and sought the opinion of the session on Campbell's offer. The elders had no difficulty in answering that in no circumstances would they consider selling any of the glebe. They had just experienced several years of inflation, and selling the glebe 'might be detrimental to the Incumbent and his Successors'. They would be willing to feu the ground, measuring almost two acres, at an annual rate of five guineas. By consent of both parties the matter went to arbitration, and Campbell eventually agreed to feu the ground.

It is pleasant to record that at this time, 1770, the kirk session had their attention drawn to the plight of Miss Jenny Lindsay, daughter of David Johnston's predecessor in the charge. This lady was lame, and as the record puts it, 'could not be in the most comfortable circumstances'. The session agreed to 'make her a compliment such as their funds would admit of' and presented her with £10 sterling, 'as a small testimony of their great regard for Mr Lindsay and his family'.

Cromwell's Citadel had remained the fashionable, residential area of North Leith. The better class of townsfolk had houses in the Citadel, with gardens, and having sold a house there in order to build the new school, the session now sought to acquire a new interest in that prestigious area, and set about building a weaver's shop there which they proposed renting at the rate of eight per cent per annum of the cost of building it. Hand-loom weaving was then in its heyday, and property was considered to be the safest form of investment, as there was then no stock exchange, and neither banking nor insurance offered attractive returns. The trade incorporations sank much of their funds in property, and about a year after the kirk session's venture in the Citadel the Society of Free Fishermen in Newhaven proposed buying property in that village. As the Free Fishermen were subject to supervision in financial matters by the kirk session, a committee of elders visited Newhaven to discuss the matter with the Boxmaster of the Fishermen and his committee. As everything appeared to be in order this purchase went ahead with the session's blessing.

Congregational singing in the Church generally was at a very low ebb, and Mr Johnston, aware of this, proposed to the session to stop the old practice of 'lining'. This was the system, originating in the days of widespread illiteracy, whereby each line of a psalm was read out by the precentor, before being sung by the people. It completely destroyed all musical form or meaning, and had long outlived any usefulness it might once have had. In April 1771 the elders heartily approved the proposal to allow the congregation to sing the psalms without the constant interruption of 'lining'. But the engrained habit of generations was difficult to change, and without a clear, strong lead from the precentor it would be a long time before there could be any change for the better. It was not until December 1775 that the session at last took the bull by the horns and decided that 'the Precentor now officiating was (thro' a defect of ear) indifferently qualified for that office'. It was the duty of the session clerk, if he himself had not the voice for it, to engage someone who could lead the singing and to pay him. James Gladstones had obviously failed to find a suitable precentor—perhaps because of the payment he was prepared to offer. The session now decided to ask Mr Johnston to find a precentor and agreed to allow the minister 20/- yearly for that purpose.

While that might seem a beggarly sum, the precentor was not called upon to do any more than lead the singing at the twice weekly services. He was given a gown by the kirk session, and could do much to enhance the standard of public worship from his desk below the pulpit. The succession of precentors serving under Dr Johnston opens a window for us on one aspect of congregational life at that period. In October 1802 the precentor resigned, and three weeks later a successor was appointed. The session were prepared to pay Andrew Lithgow £8.00 a year, provided he would take a weeknight class in church music. About the turn of the century it had dawned on several congregations in Leith that the Sunday singing might best be improved if some instruction were given during the week. So Mr Lithgow was engaged in the first instance for a six months' trial. He gave satisfaction and the engagement was made permanent on Whitsunday 1803. Nine months later the session heard that the minister had dismissed Mr Lithgow 'for improper conduct'. This time, with more caution, they appointed James Muckhart, a local man from South Leith, who handed in a certificate of his moral character from Dr Dickson, one of the ministers of South Leith. Muckhart was engaged 'providing his conduct and deportment be satisfactory to the session'.

In the spring of 1809 the kirk session decided to set up a music school 'for the improvement of psalmody in this parish'. Mr Muckhart the precentor appears to have resigned or been dismissed. The committee of session charged with organizing the music school approached an Edinburgh music publisher with a selection of thirty-seven psalm tunes, to be issued as a book for the new school. A hundred copies were ordered, to be sold for a shilling each. Mr Porteous the new precentor was to take charge of the school on Mondays and Wednesdays at 6.30 pm and no scholar was to be admitted until he or she had bought a copy of the book of tunes. The school opened midway through June 1809, and the response took the organizers aback. A month after the opening 178 pupils were attending and another 200 copies of the tune book had to be ordered. Mr Porteous was paid £8.00 per annum as precentor, and another £8.00 as teacher of the music school.

There seems to have been no idea of running the music school as a permanent feature of congregational life; the arrangement was to continue for a year, at the end of which a fresh decision on its future would be made. The elders appeared to expect that after a year or two of instruction at the school the congregational singing on Sundays would be so much improved that no more weeknight instruction would be needed.

At the end of two years the school was still catering for a very large number of pupils. No age limit was set, but the great majority of pupils were youngsters. At first practices were held in the schoolroom, but latterly the large numbers had made it necessary to use the church. The kirk session were now somewhat embarrassed by the music school. Every year a subscription was taken up throughout the parish to meet the expenses of the school. This took time and effort that might have been better spent in other ways. But with an attendance of 150 the music school could not be stopped. It was decided to continue it, but Mr Porteous applied for an increase in salary. The elders replied with an astute proposal. Instead of £8 as precentor, and £8 as teacher of the music school, the session now offered to pay him £10 in all, leaving him to make up the difference by charging his pupils at the music school a fee. In this way he might well end up much better off; and this, after all, was the way in which all private teachers in the town made a living. The arrangement was accepted, but two years later the precentor made a fresh application for an augmentation. The answer was a firm 'No', but since Mr Porteous had not been able to persuade any of his pupils to pay any fees during the past year the elders gave him two guineas in a present 'which is not to be considered as a precedent'.

Mr Porteous struggled on as precentor on his £10 a year until July 1823, when the kirk session, having received complaints about 'Mr Porteous' mode of singing', sacked him:

> and as the expence of procuring a proper singer will be considerably greater than what was given to Mr Porteous,

the Session recommend to their Committee to procure subscriptions amongst the Congregation in order to augment his salary.

The new precentor was David Hill and he was paid no less than £25 a year 'on condition that he shall teach twice a week (except in the dead of winter) the poorer classes of the congregation'.

This account of the successive precentors in North Leith illustrates the almost unbroken rise in the cost of living in the half-century from 1770 to 1820, and at the same time the very wide gap between the rich and the poor. That was the era of the building of the Edinburgh New Town, when the rich were able to separate themselves from the poor as never before. In Leith the same kind of development was taking place. Those who could afford it, and who were interested in music, had their children taught at home, and attended such concerts as were available; but those who were poor had no teacher, heard no concerts; it was the poor music lovers who attended the weeknight singing class taken by the precentor.

In the 1770s the increasing population brought a continual increase in the number of destitute poor. The poor roll was rapidly becoming unmanageable. Every possible source of money was explored for the benefit of the poor box. In 1776 Thomas Gladstones the treasurer proposed that the session should buy a set of mortcloths. The job of the modern undertaker was done by the porters, but the bulk of the population spent no money on coffins. The body was wrapped in a shroud and placed on a bier which was borne to the churchyard. To provide at least a show of decency a black mortcloth was draped over the bier for the journey to the burial-place, and these mortcloths were on hire at various prices according to the quality of the material. In earlier times, when almost all the population was connected in one way or another with one of the trade incorporations, the mortcloth was hired from the family's corporation. The money from hiring charges went to swell the funds of the corporation, which in turn were used to benefit the members. Mr Gladstones realized that many incomers to the port had no connection with any incorporation; but the only mortcloths available belonged to one or other of these bodies, who were accordingly enjoying an inflated income from hiring charges. He urged the session to invest in a set of mortcloths—fine and coarse, large and small. This was agreed, the mortcloths were purchased, and the session issued instructions that every burial in the churchyard should take place with mortcloths hired from the session, excepting for those families belonging to one or other of the incorporated societies of North Leith. At the same time the corporations were forbidden to hire their mortcloths to any other than their own members. Five shillings was to be charged for the best cloths, except for those families the treasurer thought could afford to pay more. He was told to charge these families so much as he thought they would be willing to pay. The charge for coarser cloths was 3/6d, and the small cloths, presumably for children, were to be let out for half-a-crown.

That was a good scheme, providing a small but fairly steady income, but it by no means solved the problem of how to deal with the mounting number of poor. When war with the French broke out in 1793 the cost of living was soon rising again. Shipyard workers escaped the activities of the press gang, but most of the other able-bodied men were conscripted to the forces, and many families reduced to dire poverty. In November 1800 the kirk session called a public meeting to decide what might be done to relieve distress in the parish. It was agreed to open a voluntary subscription list for the benefit of the poor, and the gentlemen present at the meeting were given the job of distributing the money collected.

This fund was only one of many expedients tried out for the relief of poverty, but none of these voluntary efforts could provide for all the poor all the time. Various wealthy and sympathetic individuals made genuine efforts to relieve distress in the parish. Free coal was distributed at Christmas, cheap oatmeal was fairly regularly available for some weeks in winter. A soup kitchen was tried out in December 1816, but it had to be restricted to 'fifty of the most necessitous persons'. And the situation at Newhaven continued to be difficult. That village community of fisher folk still distanced themselves from the rest of the parish. When the kirk session had dealt with a number of poor folk seeking help, and coming from Newhaven, the elders at last had a meeting with the officials of the Free Fishermen's Society, and pointed out to them that they had always claimed the right to look after their own poor, and on that understanding never contributed to the offering at the church door. It was made plain to the elders, however, that what the Free Fishermen meant by their poor was the poor of their own society, and not the poor of the whole village. The kirk session protested, but the Fishermen would not give way, and the argument was never resolved.

In the summer of 1817 the General Assembly sent to all parishes a 'Questionnaire on the Poor', for of course the problem of the poor was nationwide. Some facts from the answers given in the North Leith return are interesting. The annual average from church door collections amounted to £119 sterling, all of which was given to the poor. The highest rate of monthly relief in North Leith was 3/6d (17½p), and the lowest rate 2/6d (12½p). There were also those who, unemployed most of the year, could find part-time or seasonal work in the fields. These were known as the Industrious Poor, and when unemployed they received at most 1/6d (7½p) per week but the rate could be as low 8d (3p) per week. It was still the rule that three years' residence in the parish was required before anyone qualified for the Poor Roll, but there was no prohibition on begging. One or two of the questions were given misleading answers. Asked about the number of people in the parish who had not been taught to read, the answer given was 'None that we know of'. In fact many poor children never went to school. Asked again whether there were any families who, through their poverty, did not possess a Bible, it was answered, 'None, to the best of our knowledge', which again was nonsensical. The General Assembly's questions were answered only with respect to those people actively connected with the Church—and many in the town had no such connection. At the parish school the fees charged were a mere 4/- per quarter, but families on poor relief could never find that money for their children's education. The kirk session paid school fees for eight scholars, but that did not mean that every child in the parish received an elementary education.

One change that brought considerable benefit to the local poor, was a motion in the kirk session in February 1777 that in place of the long-established annual celebration of the Lord's Supper, there should in future be a bi-annual celebration, as had been instituted in South Leith, and that the two parishes should observe the sacrament on the same day. This met with unanimous approval, several elders saying they had long wished for the change. This would add considerably to the work of the minister, when all the services connected with the sacrament are remembered, but Mr Johnston expressed himself happy with the new arrangement. After a year it was found that the offerings from two communion seasons rather than one, had brought a considerable increase to the poor fund, and it was agreed to add one hundred merks to the minister's stipend. The treasurer also proposed to increase his brother the schoolmaster's salary, but this was deferred.

One of the sources for the North Leith stipend was the fish tithe of Leith and Newhaven. Originally it had been expected that the elders themselves could have these dues collected from boats arriving at or departing from the little harbours of the early seventeenth century. In the succeeding century and a half the volume of fish arriving at or passing through these ports increased enormously, and collecting the tithes was a complicated and time-consuming business. From the mid-seventeenth century the tithes were farmed out. A public roup was held annually and the tack went to the highest bidder, but in time the roup became less popular, as collecting the tithes became ever more difficult, some skippers refusing to pay, or showing great reluctance to do so. The kirk session still preferred the roup, but it became normal for a local merchant to make an offer for the tithes, which, after haggling, was agreed without a roup. In June 1775 Robert Strong offered £40 sterling, and made an agreement with the elders to pay annually at that rate for six years. Just before this arrangement was due to expire, some objectors raised an action in the Court of Session to have the fish tithes abolished, and to the consternation of the kirk session the Law Lords decided 'That all Fish exported were not liable to Teind, and likewise that all Fish which pay Teind elsewhere, are also exempted'. If these restrictions were put into effect the income to the kirk session would be much reduced, so it was determined to appeal to the House of Lords. The appeal failed, so the fish tithe was not abolished, but restricted. Some fish arriving at Leith had been landed at other ports, and may have paid local tithes at these places. Such cargoes were no longer to be liable for tithe at Leith. Some cargoes arriving at Leith were not sold locally, but were intended for export: these cargoes were also to be exempt from tithe.

For many years the firm of Robert Strong remained as tacksmen of the tithes, Robert junior succeeding his father. A new agreement was made at six-yearly intervals, but the rent offered had to rise with the general rise in costs, and by 1803 Mr Strong was paying £100 per annum for the tithes. For many years there was no more trouble, but simmering dissatisfaction over this charge remained, and came to a head again in late Victorian times.

In March 1781 the University of Edinburgh conferred on the Rev David Johnston the degree of Doctor of Divinity, to the satisfaction of the North Leith congregation, for their minister was well-known and his work approved over a much wider area than his parish. At the same time the growing industrialisation of Leith was bringing with it many social problems. By the 1780s the area around the quays and shipyards was overcrowded, although this was not yet realized as a problem. What was regarded as an intolerable nuisance was the horde of children and youngsters roaming the streets, uneducated, unemployed, uncared for, and notorious for their rags, their unwashed appearance, their filthy language, their hooliganism, their addiction to alcohol and other vices. David Johnston had been brought up in a village community, as had all his generation born and raised in North Leith. This new generation, born in slums and growing up without any home life or parental control, presented a problem that defeated the elders, accustomed to taking responsibility for the well-being of the community.

The problem, of course, was widespread, as Britain tried to come to terms with some of the side-effects of the Industrial Revolution. An original experiment had been made by Robert Raikes in Gloucester, where he opened the first Sunday School in 1780. In March 1788 the Society for Propagating Religious Knowledge among the Poor, bypassing the challenge of the Edinburgh streets, called a meeting in Leith, to which the local Presbyterian and Episcopalian ministers were invited. The meeting resolved to start a Sabbath Evening School, and get a divinity student to take charge of it. Dr Johnston put this proposal to the session:

> The Session, convinc'd that such a school by the divine blessing, may be attended with many happy consequences, appointed the Moderator to return the Society their thanks for their benevolent design, and to request that the School may be opened next Lord's Day evening, in the School house, at six o'clock, and that the Moderator may make intimation thereof from the Pulpit Sabbath first. The Session resolves that a Collection be made in the Church Sabbath se'nnight, in order to assist in some measure the Society to carry forward their laudable designs.

In the first *Statistical Account for Scotland*, published in 1793, Dr Johnston wrote that one hundred children were attending the Sabbath School in his parish:

and it is of the greatest benefit to the place; young people who formerly were brought up in the profoundest ignorance, and grossly mis-spent the Sabbath day, are now taught a reverence for it, and are educated in the principles of religion and morals. The master is allowed five guineas a year by the Society for Promoting Religious Knowledge among the Poor.

This new movement was seen by the Church as a highly commendable missionary exercise; but there could be no question of allowing the children of churchgoing families to attend these new Sabbath Schools. They were a good thing, but good for 'them' rather than 'us'. Children of church families were expected to receive instruction in the faith at home, where they would also have the example of family worship to encourage them.

The school met from six o'clock till eight on Sunday evenings and from the start attendance was never any problem. All the early reports indicate that the greatest difficulty lay in securing and maintaining control of the unruly pupils. As the children were all illiterate the lessons consisted largely of Bible stories and memory work, special attention being given to the questions and answers in a variety of catechisms. The goal appears to have been to have as many children as possible able to 'prove doctrines'. This remarkable exercise involved quoting Scripture texts, giving chapter and verse, in proof of any doctrine asked for. Even with this boring, pointless and uninteresting programme, there was no falling off in attendance. After a while, too, the remarkable band of enthusiasts who took these children in hand, realized that their pupils could not make progress without learning to read. They set out to remedy this deficiency by starting weeknight evening classes to teach reading, and many of the printed catechisms issued to the children had the alpahabet printed on the inside cover. The teachers themselves had to learn the art of handling the children without the benefit of any advice or guidance, as this was a completely novel experiment. Gradually they saw the sense of dividing the different age-groups into different classes, and the wisdom of separating boys from girls. These developments at first met strong opposition from groups and gangs determined to stay together.

It is a remarkable fact that the children attending these early Sabbath schools became for the most part reformed characters, turning from their old bad habits and uncouth behaviour, with many of them becoming respectable and successful townsfolk. There is ample evidence from outside the Sunday school movement to support this. Despite the earnest attempts to get the youngsters to 'prove doctrines' however, the most potent influence brought to bear on them was the character and personality of their Sunday school teachers. These were neither learned nor saintly; they were just interested in the youngsters, and became friendly with them. For those children their Sunday school teacher was the first adult they had ever known to offer them friendship. It was not until the 1830s that congregational Sunday schools were tried. Long before then these schools had proliferated, many elders starting a school in their own district. The difficulty lay not in finding children to attend, but in finding somewhere to meet. The movement was a very successful experiment in social welfare.

David Johnston's interests extended well beyond his congregation and parish. He had a benevolent concern for the poor, the sick, the disabled, and that concern led again and again to action, whenever the opportunity arose. In the society in which the North Leith minister lived and worked there were none of the charities and welfare bodies the twentieth century in Britain takes for granted. There were no hospitals, no pensions, no police force, no shelter or protection from the effects of accident, illness, or the burden of disability. And a society that had never known any such amenities accepted that life was hard and that nothing could be done about it. The will of God and the workings of Providence must simply be tholed.

The minister of North Leith was not content to thole. He believed Providence threw up opportunities for those who were willing to improve what was bad, and to right what was wrong. The enthusiastic supporter of the Sabbath school had eyes for much more that cried out for change. He saw blind beggars in the streets dragging out their days in misery. He believed such men and women could lead useful lives if they were placed in a situation where that would be possible. He conceived the idea of an asylum—a place of refuge—for the blind. Drumming up all the support he could get from friends, and using a good deal of his own money, he managed to establish an Asylum for the Industrious Blind in Edinburgh in 1793—a place where the blind could come and work at whatever they could put their hands to. They sold what they made and, at first they were fed on the premises. The work developed, grew and spread in a variety of ways. The present-day Royal Blind Asylum and School is the fruition of that original idea and action of David Johnston.

There was not the same widespread approbation for another charitable venture Dr Johnston plunged into ahead of his time. He became deeply concerned over the plight of unmarried mothers. A deeply hypocritical society wanted nothing to do with these unfortunate women, many of whom were innocent victims or dupes, and they could find no employment. Once again, indifferent to public opinion, David Johnston visited his philanthropic friends and managed to set up the Magdalene Asylum in the Canongate. As with the Blind Asylum, this product of David Johnston's independent thinking and single-minded activity has become an accepted and approved branch of social welfare.

On Christmas Day 1798 the kirk session met as usual, since Christmas was not kept then as any kind of holiday. At that meeting two important decisions were made: the first was that a Register of Burials should be kept. Surprisingly such a record had not hitherto existed for the parish, but the session clerk was ordered to see to the matter. A fee would be charged for each entry—not less than 3d or more than 6d—presumably at the clerk's discretion 'except the poor who are not able to afford it'. The Moderator then announced that after more than forty years in the ministry he would be glad of some assistance. The matter would appear to have been discussed unofficially for some time previously, as Dr Johnston was able to propose that Mr Walter Foggo Ireland, Preacher of the Gospel, 'with whose talents and gifts the Session and Congregation were well acquainted', should be appointed as his Assistant and Successor. The session warmly supported this proposal, and called a meeting of the inhabitants, who were, of course, the patrons of the charge, and would have to be consulted. At this public meeting, on 9 January 1799, a roll was made up of all those covered by the expression 'the haill inhabitants'. This meant the male heads of families in the parish, since no women or minors were entitled to vote. This list provides an interesting comparison between the various districts of the parish. At the head of the list are Thomas Smith, Baron Bailie of the Canongate and North Leith, the Rev Dr Johnston the minister, seventeen elders and Alexander Ross the session clerk. The heads of families then follow. In the Coalhill are 123; 'Back of ye Kirk', 33; North Leith (ie the parish area generally), 130; Citadel, 71; Newhaven, 109; Then follow single houses—Bathfield, Anchorfield, Leith Mount, Hillhousefield, the hamlet of Damhead, Cherrybank, Jessfield, Laverockbank, Lixmount, Trinity Mains, Trinity Gate, Trinity Lodge.

The meeting voted unanimously for Mr Ireland as Assistant and Successor to Dr Johnston, but not without an argument. Mr George Robertson of Hillhousefield claimed that the heritors ought to be listed separately from the rest of the community. Dr Johnston opposed this, maintaining that no heritor had any right to a vote because he was a landowner, but only as an inhabitant, in the same category as any other inhabitant. However, as this distinction would make no difference in the present election there was no need to pursue the argument, so long as his clearly stated opinion was minuted. So Mr Ireland, to the general satisfaction, became the second minister at North Leith at the age of twenty-three.

Now that he could rely on assistance Dr Johnston lost no time in bringing forward another new idea. He suggested an evening service on Sundays during the summer of 1800. Mr Ireland and he would share in the experiment. What was proposed was an evening lecture. This was not a sermon, but rather a Bible lesson, in which the minister read a passage of scripture, explaining the meaning and commenting as he went along. At an earlier period, with widespread illiteracy and a dearth of Bibles among the people, the lecture was a part of every Sunday service. The lecture had dropped out of regular use, so this was a proposal to revive an old practice. The elders welcomed the idea, 'which might particularly be a means of preventing unnecessary walking on the evening of the Lord's Day, and resolved to begin on Sabbath next'. The series ran from May to mid-October. Winter evening services were not practicable, with the need to heat and light the church, and people reluctant to walk out in the dark, which was not only disagreeable, but dangerous for the elderly, with no street lighting and no pavements.

The country had now been at war with France for eight years. Every ablebodied man not in some occupation necessary to the country's good, was serving in the Forces, the cost of living was rising again, and on 23 June 1801 a collection was taken at Church on behalf of 'the Widows and Orphans of those who fell in the late engagement in Egypt'. This was the Battle of Alexandria, fought on 21 March that year, in which the Forty-second Highlanders (the Black Watch) were engaged. That collection yielded £20 sterling.

It was then, which might well have been thought a most unpromising time, that the idea of building a new church was mooted:

> The Session taking into consideration that the Church is a great deal too small for the Parish, and being desirous of having a larger one built if a proper place could be

procured, were informed that that piece of Ground in the Citadel which was fewed some years ago by the Minister and Kirk Session to the late Mr John Scougal was soon to be sold, which would be a very convenient situation, they impowered the Ministers, the Treasurer, Col. Rimington, Mr Strong, Mr Couper and Mrs Young to attend the sale and go such a length for the Purchase as they think it is worth.

At the next session meeting it was announced that the ground had been acquired for £140 sterling. The minister in fact had attended the sale, persuaded other potential bidders to refrain from bidding as the church needed the ground, and bought it for the upset price. Then Dr Johnston, probably aware that the work now envisaged might involve the session in long and complicated legal procedures, suggested that it would be to their advantage to have a lawyer on the kirk session. He proposed inviting James Moncrieff, Advocate, son of the Rev Sir Henry Moncrieff of St Cuthbert's, to become an elder, as he was a heritor, living in the parish for most of the year. Mr Moncrieff was ordained as an elder on 6 December, and this is the first occasion on which an elder in North Leith is recorded as having been ordained rather than elected or admitted. A committee was then chosen to procure plans for a new church building to seat from 1600 to 1800 people.

It was in this year, 1801, that the first national census was ordered—the first of the series taken at ten-yearly intervals, which still continues. Each successive census has included more detailed information than its predecessor. This first numbering of the people in North Leith was engrossed in the session records, for the act ordering the census provided that in each parish the schoolmaster would be responsible for the count, and that a copy of his findings should be preserved and passed to his successor. The parish schoolmaster in North Leith was also the session clerk, and he reported to the session that 'after much labour and enquiry at every house in the parish' he had completed his report.

The population of North Leith in October 1801 totalled 3228 souls—1355 males and 1873 females. This was exclusive of men then in the Army or Royal Navy. Six were employed in agriculture, 381 in Trade or Mechanics, and 2904 otherwise. Six employed in agriculture is misleading, as this figure represented only those employed full-time in farming. In fact a considerable number of the 2904 'otherwise employed' were seasonal farm workers, not regularly employed, but taken on at busy times for haymaking and harvesting oats and barley, Women were employed in weeding, and gangs brought in to hoe turnips and bring in potatoes.

Dr Johnston was quite right in supposing there might be legal complications arising from the proposal to built a new church. The Canongate Magistrates, who owned the superiority of the ground on which the old church stood, heard of the proposed new church, and indicated they would like some conversation on the subject before the matter was advanced any further. The committee of the kirk session met with the magistrates, and after much talk the elders were asked to state their case in a Memorial. This was done by Dr Johnston describing the origin and historical background of the present church, and explaining that, as the building was now too small to serve the parish, a new church, holding twice as many as the present one, would answer the need of the parish, and that as there was no money available for such a project it would be necessary to sell the present church and manse.

This memorial was sent to the magistrates, desiring an answer at their early convenience—but no answer was made. After waiting a considerable time the committee of session again called on the magistrates. To their astonishment the magistrates claimed to own all the seats in the church, and that as they had been in the habit of holding magistrates' courts in the session house *ex gratia*, the session would be obliged to build a new court-house. Moreover, if the old church were sold, the purchaser would be obliged to pay 1% of the purchase money annually to the Canongate Magistrates as feu duty. All of this was reported to a meeting of the inhabitants, and it was agreed to take the matter to the Court of Session, where they should seek a Declarator of their right to sell the church. In the meantime a committee was appointed to consult the early minutes of the session to clear up several points which were in doubt. This committee, unfortunately, had to report that such of the minutes as they could read gave no information on the matter at issue, but that for the most part they just could not read the handwriting of those early minutes. They would now leave it to the session whether any steps should be taken to have them deciphered. In the meantime Counsel's opinion had been sought and, guided by this, the session, instead of raising an action, decided to approach the Solicitor General to act as arbiter between them and the magistrates.

As the magistrates were unwilling to submit the question to arbitration the kirk session went to the Court of Session and in June 1804 that court found in their favour. This was the first hurdle crossed. Dr Johnston next wrote to the various incorporations, enclosing a copy of the plan for the new church, and seeking their reactions. This was a difficult area for negotiation. The incorporations all had their own seats in the old church, and would have to be similarly accommodated in the new building. Unlike the situation in the neighbouring parish of South Leith, however, the North Leith corporations were not independent bodies, but merely branches of the Canongate corporations. Whatever was decided in North Leith would be subject to the agreement of the parent bodies in Canongate. The replies from the corporations were mixed. One or two accepted the proposals; some accepted with certain provisions; others wished more details to be made clear. Trinity House was on a different footing, as the officials at their convening-house in the Kirkgate were all local men. But the discussions with Trinity House were at this stage the most long drawn-out and indecisive.

The whole project for building a new church now became bogged down. On 30 July 1804 the church and manse were exposed for sale at the Assembly Rooms in Leith, but failed to find a purchaser. The heritors, who owned nothing of the church, but whose agreement and financial backing would be necessary to pay for the new building, did nothing. Meetings with them were repeatedly postponed. Time passed, the war continued, Trafalgar was fought and won, and the varied life of the parish kept the elders busy.

Young Walter Ireland, appointed as Dr Johnston's assistant and successor, had no security of tenure. He boarded with Dr Johnston, who presumably charged him nothing, but as he was not the parish minister he received no stipend. The senior minister was quite well off, as North Leith was now paying one of the best stipends in the country, and from 1793 he had also enjoyed a small pension as a Chaplain-in-Ordinary to the King. On 24 June 1806 'The Session allowed twenty pounds to Mr Ireland as a present in Consideration of his being Dr Johnston'a Assistant, and ordered the Treasurer to pay him that sum'. Year by year thereafter the session paid Mr Ireland what they could afford, always stressing that this was 'a present', and did not bind them in any way to continue these payments.

An extraordinary situation arose in the spring of 1807. Someone pointed out to the kirk session that they did not have a valid title to the ground they had bought in 1801 with a view to building the new church there. No name is mentioned, but it is possible that James Moncrieff the advocate, ordained as an elder in 1801, was the man responsible for bringing the matter to light. It was pointed out that the land in question was part of the minister's glebe, which ought never to have been put on the market. The session had spent £140 buying ground which in fact belonged to the minister! Both the kirk session and the minister seem to have been ignorant as to the bounds of the glebe, although the stipend derived in part from glebe rent. After discussion it was agreed that in order to spare the session's funds from loss, Dr Johnston should buy the ground from the session for the price they had paid for it, plus a sum to cover the expenses the session had incurred, and the legal costs of the present transaction. A disposition was then

The present Minister, the Reverend Alistair McGregor.

Abbot Ballantynes Bridge built shortly before 1493. A chapel was built at the north (*left*) end—the first North Leith Church.

The original North Leith Church at Quayside, off Coburg Street.

The new North Leith Church after its opening in 1816.

Two Communion tokens from North Leith Church
(*front and back views*) dated 1816 and 1843.

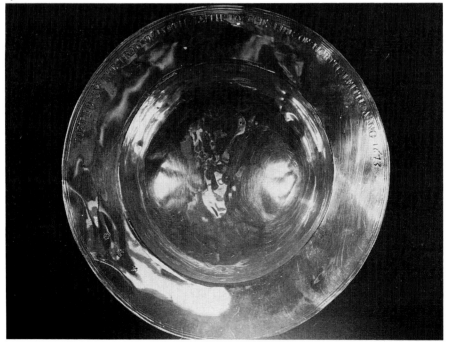

The North Leith Silver Baptismal bowl, still in use today, with inscription:
'*gifted by the Treds of North Leith to the Kirk of North Leith: Anno 1673.*'

Interior of North Leith Church after its renovation in 1920.

Interior of the Church after its renovation between 1948 and 1950.

Ministers of North Leith Church from 1765 to 1986 (*reading clockwise from bottom left*): Alexander Davidson, William Smith, Robert Stewart, Andrew Wallace Williamson, John McCulloch, James R S Wilson, Hugh O Douglas, John H Gibson, A Stewart Todd, Douglas Clarke and William G Neill surrounding the bust of Dr David Johnston.

The former Bonnington Church in Summerside Street, demolished in 1970.

The former North Leith Free Church, St Ninians Church on Ferry Road, demolished 1987.

The Burning Bush stone above the entrance to the existing North Leith Church Hall, dating from 1843, and brought from St Ninians Church before its final demolition.

The North Leith Church Hall dedicated and opened on 11 December 1987.

The present Kirk Session of North Leith Church in the Session House
(*for names see* Appendix II).

drawn up in the session's name conveying the ground to Dr Johnston.

With the delay in proceeding with the new building, various interested parties had time to consider how the change might affect them. The incorporations owned seats in the church which they did not require for their own members. As the church was too small for the parish there had for some years been an increasing demand for seats, and the corporations rented their spare seats to the kirk session, who in turn offered them to the parish for seat rent. The Shoemakers of Canongate now proposed to renew their lease of seats to the session for nineteen years at £4—a substantial increase on previous years. The session rejected this as exorbitant, and Dr Johnston wrote the incorporation to that effect, offering £3 annually, and warning that if the Shoemakers did not accept that the kirk session could prevent the corporation renting the seats to anyone else. At this period, frustrated by the increasingly complicated situation that was developing over the proposed new church there seemed to be a bitter edge to the session's public relations. There was a dispute with a builder over the development of a site adjacent to the parish school, which the session claimed was an encroachment on their property. Again, in quite a different area of interest the novelty of the evening services had apparently worn off, and in April 1807, at the beginning of a new summer series, it was decided that if attendances did not improve the project would be discontinued.

One consequence of the escalation of the population was the difficulty of maintaining any effective church discipline. Dr Johnston was concerned with the growing laxity in Sabbath observance; and an increasing number of people with little or no church connection were asking baptism for their children. The minister therefore got the session to agree that any application for baptism in future should be accompanied by a certificate from the elder of their district that they 'were circumspect in their walk, and regular in attending public worship'. The session then had an engraving made for a form of baptismal certificate—1000 copies were ordered in the first instance, at a cost of £4.15.

The business of the new church advanced slowly. It was now nine years since the matter had first been discussed by the elders, but on 16 November 1810 the heritors met in the church and agreed that a new church might be erected on a site in the area bounded by the Queensferry Road, North Fort Street, Albany Street and Couper Street—the exact location to be agreed with the kirk session. This was material progress. From this time on the work went smoothly enough, though still slowly. A site was agreed, a careful examination of the funds available for the building was reported to the kirk session, and finally, on 11 April 1814 the foundation stone of the new church was laid by Dr Johnston. With the stone were deposited the coins of the realm and the newspapers of the day. On the stone itself an elaborate inscription was set out:

BY THE BLESSING OF ALMIGHTY GOD
IN THE 53rd YEAR OF THE REIGN OF THE MOST
EXCELLENT PRINCE

GEORGE III

The old church of North Leith
erected in 1606
Having become incommodious for the population
of the parish

DAVID JOHNSTON D.D. minister of the
parish, & one of His Majesty's Chaplains for Scotland
amidst the acclamations of a great concourse of people,
laid the foundation stone of this new intended Fabric,
dedicated to the Glory, and set apart to the worship of

THE ONE TRUE GOD, and
OUR ONLY SAVIOUR
JESUS CHRIST

on the Eleventh Day of April,
In the year of our Lord 1814,
And of the Era of Masonry 5814
Dr Johnston being in the eightieth year of

his age, and the Forty-ninth of his ministry
in the parish

WALTER FOGGO IRELAND, D.D.
his Assistant and Successor

And the Committees who at the unanimous desire of the Parish,
Begun & Perfected the Arrangement of this great Undertaking being

For the Heritors

Robert Menzies, shipbuilder in Leith, Convener
Robert Liddell, manager of the Edr & Leith Shipping Co. Ltd.
Archibald Cleghorn, merchant, Leith
John Glover, wright in Leith
Archibald Ronaldson, butcher in Leith
Alexr Neilson Lamb, solicitor at law, Leith
Peter Couper, Writer to the Signet

For the Kirk Session

David Johnston, D.D., convener
Walter Foggo Ireland, D.D.
Robert Douglas, kirk treasurer
Alexr Goalen, late shipbuilder, Leith
David Auchinleck, gardener, Newhaven
Henry Paterson, wright, Hillhousefield
Alexr Gray, wright in Leith

William Burn, architect in Edr
having furnished the plan,
And John Russell, builder in Leith
being Contractor for building & finishing the Church.

As the Foundation has been laid in Concord,
may the Cope Stone be brought forth with Joy.

At the first meeting of session after the foundation stone was laid it was proposed to make the usual 'present' to Mr (now Dr) Ireland, but on this occasion he declined it with thanks:

as by a late arrangement with Dr Johnston, he was now in receipt of the one half of the produce of the feus of the Glebe of North Leith, and he felt it a duty incumbent upon him respectfully to decline any further aid from the funds of the session.

But other matters pressing for attention were by no means as pleasant. The churchyard had given cause for anxiety, ever since the site was given to the church in 1664 to replace the old graveyard taken over by the soldiers who built Cromwell's Citadel. Its position on the river bank was always at risk from erosion when the river was in spate. Added to this, with the growing demand for berths in the harbour through the increase in trade from the mid-eighteenth century, the wharfage along the Shore was quite inadequate for the vessels crowding in, so over the years, boats unable to find berths in the harbour were tying up alongside the churchard dyke. In 1802 the treasurer had complained of the dangerous practice of boats at the churchyard casting their anchors among the graves. As he rightly said, this was not only indecent, but was likely to damage the churchyard wall, which was known to be none too secure. The session promptly put a stop to that practice. Another ongoing struggle was carried on against local housewives using the churchyard as a bleaching green. It was not normal domestic practice then to have a weekly wash-day. The water supply in Leith was always inadequate, and without even the basic facility of piped water, far less hot water, washing was postponed until the large quantity of soiled linen justified a whole day being spent bringing stoups of water from the public well, heating a boiler and washing. Then space was needed for drying and bleaching the clothes. On a fine spring day every inch of the churchyard might well be covered with clothes bleaching—a sight which gave the elders no pleasure. But that was a minor irritant compared with what happened in the spring of 1809 when, after heavy rain, a great stretch of the churchyard dyke fell into the river. The treasurer said this had happened more than once in the past, and that the usual procedure was to pay for the repairs by taking up a subscription throughout the parish. This time the damage was more extensive than before, but the same method was adopted.

Two years later the wall was damaged again, and the session protested to Edinburgh town council that their shoremaster was to blame, in allowing a ship to be moored at the churchyard wall, and so causing the damage. The town council replied that it was not the ship, but the effect of erosion that was affecting the wall; but they promised to bear half the expense of repairs if the session would have the job done at once. This gave general satisfaction, but the churchyard continued to give cause for concern. In March 1819 a ploughman in a field south-west of the new kirk uncovered a bag containing a bloodstained sheet, a rope with a quantity of human hair adhering to it, and a small type of boathook. The elders agreed this was evidence of body-snatching from the churchyard, which was not an uncommon crime at that period. A public meeting was called and a rota system was agreed for the watching of the kirkyard by volunteers.

In view of the impending completion of the new church building, and the need to pay the various tradesmen, it was of urgent importance to sell the old church and manse for a good price. The properties were exposed to public roup and sale on 8 May 1816 at the upset price of £1500. The time was most unpropitious: the long war with France had ended at Waterloo just eleven months previously, and the country was at once plunged into industrial depression. During more than twenty years of war the port of Leith had prospered, as it was the only Scottish port from which convoys sailed, so foreign traders almost inevitably had to use the facilities at Leith. The end of the war changed all that. There was massive unemployment; ships were laid up; trading through the port dwindled and property values slumped. The heritors of North Leith—business and professional men—realized that the sale of the old church would be difficult, so they agreed that between them, they would buy the properties at the upset price, or, if there were any other bids, they would go as far as £2000. The nine heritors involved arranged to provide the money in various proportions of one, two, four or five shares each. Their plan was to hold the properties until such time as prices might improve, when they could dispose of their holding at a profit.

. This turned out a disaster for them. The economy was still in inflation, and the new church cost £15,000—far above the original estimates. The sale of the old church only brought in £1820, and even more depressing was the realization that had the sale not been postponed for several years, owing to various lawsuits pursued by various parties, the sale might well have yielded £4000 or £5000. The total amount of money the kirk session was able to put into the new church was £2420, and the heritors had to find the rest of the £15,000.

The new proprietors of the old church and manse were promised entry at the beginning of August 1816; it would therefore be most convenient if the new church could be opened on the first Sunday in August. By that date the premises were complete and ready to be used: unfortunately the incorporations, Trinity House and the heritors were still in dispute with the kirk session over the allocation of seats in the new building, and had called in the Sheriff of Edinburgh as arbiter. Basically the bodies owning pews in the old church wanted the same proportion of seats in the new church as they had had in the old building. The kirk session resisted this, declaring that the extra accommodation was meant for the parish as a whole rather than the incorporations. There was also argument over the relative value of seats in different parts of the church.

In the event the church was opened on Sunday 1 September. A week before the opening it was agreed that the bell for public worship would begin to ring at twenty to eleven forenoon and at two o'clock afternoon, and continue ringing for quarter of an hour 'as usual'. The session also decided that their future meetings take place in the session house at the new church. A clockmaker was employed to wind and service 'the Clock and timepiece' which doubtless referred to the new steeple clock and the clock on the front of the west gallery. Dr Johnston preached at the morning service and presented twelve Bibles for the use of the elders in their seat in the new church.

It was an exciting time. The congregation must have been

immensely proud of William Burn's magnificent church, with its spire soaring heavenwards in the midst of an area of new housing. Richard Gillone was appointed bellman, to ring the church bell at six every morning and eight in the evening, and at the usual times for public worship on the Lord's day. For this he would be paid 6/8d per month. Henry Reid, the session officer and beadle, had his annual salary of £5.00 doubled. The dispute over seating was by no means over. The longer the argument continued the more complicated it seemed to become. It was September 1817 before the Sheriff of Edinburgh issued his conclusions. Regarding the seats due to be allocated to the kirk session for letting to the congregation:

> He finds that in allocating to the kirk session of North Leith that portion of the church to which they have been found entitled, the same ought to be taken from Various parts of the Church, and from seating of different values, so as nearly as may be to put the kirk session in possession of one-sixth of the best seating of the church, one-sixth of the worst, and one-sixth of the intermediate description.

While this long dispute was annoying, the minister and session were at the same time aware that the incorporations counted for much less in the community than in former days. In the much larger population it was no longer possible to insist that every tradesman must belong to his incorporation. These bodies were increasingly being ignored, and they were legally abolished in 1846. In the meantime they could still insist on their property rights in the church, but their old influence was rapidly dissipating. Of more importance was the fact that the dearer priced seats in the new church were not being taken up. People who formerly had taken two seats in the old church were now only renting one, and others were not taking seats at all.

Not only were the greatly increased number of new seats not being rented, but it was suspected that a number of former members were now attending the new Burgher Church in Coburg Street. The presence of an alternative church in the parish had not so far been any problem to the parish kirk. South Leith had had a different experience. From the late seventeenth century South Leith had had two Episcopalian congregations—Jurors and Non-jurors—united towards the end of the eighteenth century. From 1740 there had been a group, a rapidly growing group, of Seceders. Later in the eighteenth century a Methodist congregation, and also a body of Glasites. No doubt these various sects and denominations had drawn some adherents from North Leith, but at least there were no centres for their worship in the parish. In 1788 however, the Seceders had divided into Anti-Burghers, who went to worship in St Andrew Street, and Burghers, who remained in their little church in the Carters' yard in the Kirkgate. In 1816, as the new North Leith church was being opened, the Burghers divided, the North Leith members forming their own congregation. This division may have been timed deliberately just then, as it was known the old St Ninian's Kirk was likely to be available. As soon as that building was vacated the Burghers rented it from the North Leith heritors, who were the new owners. But this was only a temporary home. Almost at once the growing Burgher congregation began building a church for themselves in Coburg Street, and the treasurer of the parish kirk was viewing these new neighbours with a calculating eye. He got permission from the session to lower the rents of the dearer seats:

> as unless this is done, the Heritors' and Kirk Session's interests will be deeply affected ... Attention to this subject is of peculiar importance at present, as if the seats are not lowered before Whitsunday, a great proportion of the parishioners will in all likelihood take seats in the Burgher meeting-house that is now building.

After the opening of the new church Dr Johnston retired. This fact was never mentioned, and would never have been admitted by Dr Johnston or anyone else. There was no conception of official retirement. Ministers, like other men, continued in active work as long as they were able. Eventually they would no longer be able for any work, but there was no idea that a man might decide at a certain age or date that he would work no more. Dr Johnston still preached occasionally, and still moved around the parish visiting, but Dr Ireland was now effectively moderator of the session and minister of the charge. There was an atmosphere of change—a feeling that with the move to the new church things would never be the same again. Society was changing, attitudes were altering. Signs of the times appeared in the session's business. In October 1820, approaching the autumn sacramental season, the session considered that attendance at the sermon on the Tuesday following the sacrament had of late years become very thin. It was decided to give up the Tuesday service in future. The old severity of kirk discipline was gradually, if reluctantly, easing. In that same autumn Mr Auchinleck, the elder from Newhaven, reported that a flagrant profanation of the Lord's day had taken place by the sailing of steamboats from Newhaven on that sacred day. Steamboats were new; this may have been their first appearance at Newhaven. Many seafaring folk thought steamboats were a novelty that would not last, but the steamers were not dependent on wind and tide in the way that sailing craft were. But novelty or not, these steamboats must observe the Lord's day like other ships. The session protested to the presbytery evidently without effect, for Mr Auchinleck was back protesting a year later.

The neighbouring parishes of North and South Leith had always been on close and friendly terms, but towards the end of 1820 they came near to a serious dispute. A Leither, Mr Ogilvy, had emigrated and made good in Canada, and, typical of Leithers in every generation, he retained the kindliest memories of his native place. When he died in Montreal he left £200 to the poor of Leith. As in his young days he had lived in South Leith the kirk session of that parish claimed to be the sole recipients of the legacy. The North Leith treasurer heard what was afoot however, and lodged a caveat, which prevented the disbursement of the money until North Leith's claim had been heard. North Leith session held that 'the poor of Leith' meant the poor of both parishes. In support of this claim they cited the fact that recently a 'carriage for the poor sick' had been bought for Leith—the whole of Leith. This was a forerunner of the modern ambulance, and the cost had been borne by the two neighbouring congregations, South Leith paying two-thirds and North-Leith one-third. On that basis North Leith claimed one-third of the Ogilvy legacy. To this the South Leith session answered that they still believed the late Mr Ogilvy by 'the poor of Leith' had meant the poor of his own native parish, yet they would be willing to let North Leith have a quarter of the legacy. Regarding the payment for the 'carriage for the poor sick', they had never been consulted. This charge had been imposed on Leith. North Leith accepted the quarter, no doubt because, in relation to the relative size of the population in both parishes, this was really a generous offer, although it was accompanied by the condition that it should be no precedent for the future.

The census of 1821 showed the population of North Leith at just over 7000. Post-war depression, unemployment and high prices took their toll to the extent that 110 paupers were receiving monthly pensions from the kirk session, and these payments to adults also had to provide for sixty-seven children whose mothers were in receipt of widows' pensions. It was a formidable total. Every case was assessed separately, but 3/- or 4/- a month was the normal subsistence rate for adults. Another one or two shillings might be allowed for children. The reasons for paupers being on the poor roll were only given in general terms—Debility, Infirmity, Ill health, Lame, Blind, Sore leg, Mental debility and so on. Widows as often as not were accepted without any specific reason given beyond the fact of their widowhood. Some children were orphans with no family support; an infant was described as 'abandoned by father and mother'. One woman was added as a presumed widow, her husband having been wrecked at sea some months previously and not heard of again. A family of four young children were destitute when their mother died while their father was still in the army. When all this could happen in the small community of North Leith, the size of the national problem presented by the destitute, before the Government accepted any responsibility, can only be imagined.

The kenspeckle figure of Dr Johnston was still to be seen about the place. He continued to dress in the style common in his younger days. His hair was curled and powdered, and he wore knee-breeches and buckled shoes, with black silk stockings in summer and fine woollen ones in winter. When fashions changed rather quickly in the early years of the nineteenth century, Robert Douglas, one of the elders, who liked to be in the fashion, turned up at a session meeting in trousers. The minister was scornful of this new-fangled style of dress. 'Robert Douglas, what d'ye mean, buskin yersel in laddie's claes? D'ye think that'll mak ye look ony younger?' Dr Johnston was no kind of doddering ancient, however; he was an athletic man all his days and walked very rapidly. Before the advent of modern competitive games, walking was a popular exercise, and Dr Johnston excelled in this. In 1816, at the age of eighty-two, he walked from Edinburgh to Glasgow in a day, to visit his daughter and son-in-law—a distance of forty-four miles! Umbrellas were introduced when he was in middle life, but he would never use one.

Another anecdote of Dr Johnston is worth recording. He went to London in 1812 to baptize a grandchild. He made the journey by stagecoach—an ordeal lasting three days and two nights. While in the city he was invited to court where, it was indicated, he would be invested as a knight. On the day before the great occasion the nobleman who was to present him sent word that the levee had been postponed for a fortnight. David Johnston refused to wait. He did not fancy another two weeks' idleness in the big city, and he certainly was not going to the expense and fatigue of the journey to Edinburgh and back again in a fortnight. So he never became Sir David.

His portrait by Sir Henry Raeburn was reckoned as a considerable achievement, not so much by the artist, but by Dr Johnston's son-in-law in Glasgow. The minister had a prejudice against having his portrait painted, for he could not put up with the necessity of sitting to the artist. His son-in-law brought back from a business trip to Paris a fine engraving of Napoleon, which he hung over the dining-room mantelpiece. When Dr Johnston visited the house and saw the picture in that place of honour he was furious and ordered his son-in-law to remove it at once. The young man answered he would remove it just as soon as he had a portrait of Dr Johnston to hang in its place—and so Sir Henry Raeburn was commissioned, and the reluctant and impatient minister had to sit still while the work was completed.

His latter years were lonely, for there was no one in the manse save himself and two servants. On 5 July 1824, ninety years of age, after fifty-nine years at North Leith, he died, and as the session minute says, 'Never was a Pastor more beloved by his Flock; Never a Pastor more deserving of a People's affection and esteem'. The funeral to North Leith churchyard was attended by about five hundred gentlemen, and the path to the grave was lined by the men and boys of the Asylum for the Industrious Blind.

In the course of his long ministry Dr Johnston became one of the best-known men in Edinburgh. He was a contemporary of the great figures of the Scottish Enlightenment, and in that comparatively small coterie of the educated and gifted citizens of the capital he knew, or at least rubbed shoulders with, many of those whose talents and achievements have assured their names a permanent place in Scottish history. He was a friend of Sir Henry Moncrieff, the minister of St Cuthbert's, who led the Evangelical party in the Kirk—the 'High Fliers' as they were derisively known. He could have met Robert Burns when the poet was in the city, and he was probably acquainted with Sir Walter Scott from his early days as an Edinburgh lawyer. For North Leith his passing marked the end of an old way of life. The idiosyncracies and mannerisms and outlook of Dr Johnston's time were to be vastly changed in the next generation, and to have known Dr Johnston became in time a note of distinction among the older generation who survived into a very different age.

CHAPTER 5

The Kirk in a Changing Parish

The comparatively short period of nineteen years from the death of Dr Johnston to the Disruption of the Church of Scotland covered some immense changes in the parish, the town and the country. During that time the management of the docks and harbour was taken from the City of Edinburgh and a Dock Commission set up which, with some changes, remained the controlling body in the port until the establishment of the Forth Ports Authority in the mid-twentieth century. In 1832 the Reformed Parliament brought into existence the Leith District of Burghs, whereby Leith, together with Portobello and Musselburgh, shared a Member of Parliament. It as not until fifty years later that the port acquired its own member. In 1833 Leith became an independent burgh, freed from the frustrations and aggravations of Edinburgh's inept and inefficient management of the port. Ten years later the Disruption split the Kirk. This was an ecclesiastical revolution which sent shock waves through the whole country, felt the more keenly in North Leith in that the parish was then vacant.

No lack of excitement, then, in public life, as the ground was steadily being built up all around the new kirk. The session heard in 1825 that the heritors had succeeded in selling the old church, which would in future be put to commercial use. There had been an agreement with the heritors that when the sale took place the clock and bells in the steeple would be reserved, as would be the clock in the church mounted on the front of the gallery opposite the pulpit. As it was not proposed to use the steeple in the redevelopment of the building, it was agreed that the steeple clock and bells should remain where they were for the time being, but the clock from inside the church was removed to the new session house.

The churchyard continued to give concern. A Society for Watching the Churchyard was formed in 1825 with the kirk session's sanction, and in the following spring a Watch House was built for the sum of £10, to give the watchers shelter. Members of the Society were available for a fee, to watch the graves of those recently buried, but after some months the session heard complaints from the neighbours that when the watch came to an end in the early hours of the morning, they fired off their guns and woke the neighbourhood. The session then ruled that instead of firing off the charge, the guns should be quietly unloaded.

Dr Ireland died on 18 February 1828 and, before proceeding to fill the vacancy the kirk session examined a statement of the stipend. This, which was taken from the papers Dr Ireland left, appears to be the first stated record of what was a complicated matter. The stipend was derived from several sources. First, from seven different heritors came corn tithes, each amounting to so many bushels and firlots of barley. The money value of these tithes varied according to the fiars prices each year, but on an average price of 25/- per bushel this portion of the stipend could be expected to yield £101.15.11 per annum. Next came the feu of the main part of the glebe, worth 231 bushels, bringing in £288.15. Further lots of glebe land paid £131.14.6. There was also £60 paid by the heritors in lieu of a manse, for since Dr Johnston's death there was no manse. The old manse, contiguous to the kirk, had been sold with it as one property. Fish tithes were a constant source of trouble. It was claimed by the lessee that they only yielded £175 per annum, but the kirk treasurer thought they ought to produce £200. Then part of the parish of North Leith had originally been taken from the West Kirk parish (St Cuthbert's), and nineteen small feu duties from various pieces of land from the West Kirk parish brought in £22.14.11½. The grand total of stipend amounted to £805.0.4½. In addition, some parts of the glebe had either not been feued, or the feuars had failed to pay their dues, and it was suggested that a notional figure of £81 might be added to the stipend if purchasers could be found for the vacant lots. All in all North Leith was paying one of the highest stipends in Scotland at that period, which was a far cry from the state of the parish when it was first erected in 1606.

Churchyard charges were reviewed in 1829, and a new scale of fees introduced. There were three classes of funeral—Hearse Funerals, Shoulder High, and Spoke Funerals. The names are descriptive. Shoulder High Funerals had no hearse, the body in the coffin being carried to the graveside on the shoulders of four bearers; and Spoke Funerals, for the poorest folk, saw the corpse in a shroud, slung between two spokes and carried by two bearers. Children, of whom there were many, were cheaper. Bearers' fees for adults were 5/-, 4/-, or 3/-, and for children, 3/- or 2/-. The standard grave was five feet deep, but could be made to a greater depth for an extra charge. A fee was charged for recording the funeral—2/6d, 1/6d or 1/-. Turfs for the graves—an obligatory charge—cost 10/- for adults and 5/- for children. The best mortcloth in a Hearse Funeral cost 21/-, but only 11/6d for shoulder-high. A cheaper cloth for a Spoke Funeral cost 8/-, and cloths for children were 3/-. These dues included fees for grave-diggers—1/- for adults and 6d for children. At the same time the kirk session, apparently for the first time, proposed that children dying unbaptized, and also stillborn children, should have their burials recorded, and that the Society of Fishermen in Newhaven should continue 'as formerly' to give the session clerk a note of burials in Newhaven churchyard. Also the practice of erecting headstones had greatly increased since the beginning of the nineteenth century, and the accumulation of these stones was becoming a nuisance. In an attempt to reduce the number of new stones it was decided to increase the fee for erection from two to five guineas, and to charge ten guineas for a horizontal stone.

In November 1829 'The session agreed that it was necessary to divide the parish into districts and to allocate the districts amongst the elders.' This reads rather oddly, as if there had not previously been elders' districts, or as if the kirk session in 1829 had no knowledge of any such previous arrangement. The last mention of the subject in the records was in 1724, when the parish was divided into nine 'quarters', two of which covered Newhaven. In the course of the next century the small village community of North Leith had been transformed into an industrial town. The old arrangement of 'quarters' had probably been allowed to stand because the constantly growing population took away the sense of stability in the community, and the anxiety and excitement of the move to the new church had given this matter a low priority. A total of thirteen districts was now agreed, and an elder appointed to each.

One important matter was reported on 26 January 1830:

> Mr Scotland (session clerk) represented to the session that a volume of the Session Register of Marriages from 1706 to 1783 had never come into his possession, that he understood they (sic) had been lent to Dr Ireland. Mr Scotland was authorised to write to Dr Ireland's executors.

No more was heard of the missing volume (or volumes), which included most of the North Leith regular marriages in the eighteenth century.

Dr Ireland's successor, the Rev James Buchanan, was settled in the charge in September 1828, but at the presbytery meeting in the previous July, when the call came up for consideration, there was a rather bizarre episode. The presentation was laid on the table by James Wyld, who must have had some difficulty in doing so. It carried some 1200 signatures, all on one sheet of paper forty feet long and four feet broad! Mr Peter Couper (whose name is preserved in Couper Street), then got up and protested. He said he was a heritor in the parish and had attended the public meeting which agreed to present Mr Buchanan. Couper stated that among those signing the call were females, and also minors of twelve years of age. He claimed many females aged twelve or thirteen, servants, and even people who did not reside in the parish had all signed. He himself had nothing against Mr Buchanan, and cordially assented to the presentation, but maintained many of the signatures were illegal: only those who were heritors, elders, or male heads of families in the parish were entitled to sign. The matter was discussed then, and at the following presbytery meeting, but it was decided to take no action, as the call, apart from the signatures objected to, was warm and harmonious.

The want of a manse was the only drawback to this desirable parish, and while Mr Buchanan seemed content with the £60 paid in lieu, the kirk session was not happy with the situation. At the annual meeting of heritors and elders in October 1830 the matter came up in a roundabout way. The churchyard had always been unsatisfactory from its proximity to the river, and the continuing effects of erosion. Everyone tried to get ground in the higher part of the graveyard, where there was now intolerable overcrowding, and a proposal was made to the meeting to turn the area surrounding the new church into a graveyard. David Davidson spoke for other elders when he protested against this. The land surrounding the new church had been bought with the intention of building thereon a church, manse and school-house. So far only the church had been built, but the intention remained and the land must not be used for any other purpose.

With regard to the old churchyard however, it was now borne in on the kirk session that living in a growing town brought burdens unknown to the former village community:

Police Office, Leith, Novr 23rd 1831.

Sir, As the notice sent you regarding the repairing of the Footpath along the churchyard wall in Coburg Street has not been attended to, I am directed to inform you that the

Commissioners will assuredly cause the needful to be done unless completed by you in the course of the present week. I am, Sir, Your very obedt servt.

(signed) J. G. Denovan.

A body of thirty Police Commissioners had been formed following an Act of Parliament in 1771 designed to provide the port with proper street lighting, cleansing, and a water supply. None of these amenities then existed in Leith. The term 'Police' had no connection with crime: policing meant taking responsibility for public amenities, with an eye especially to cleanliness and safety. The Commissioners, however, were not provided with any income, and they instituted a town tax to remedy this. Even so, the money accruing from the tax was quite insufficient for the kind of developments seen to be necessary, and even after fifty years a great deal remained to be done. When Leith became an independent burgh the work of the Police Commissioners was taken over by the town council. A police force in the modern sense was established in Leith under the Third Police Act of 1826, and the J G Denovan who signed the above letter was the Superintendent of Police. The Commissioners had at long last managed to provide for having the streets scavenged at fairly regular intervals, a rudimentary supply of piped water was laid in some parts of the town, and a number of oil lamps had been fixed at points known to be dangerous after dark— a system gradually being replaced by gas about this period. Now the Commissioners were tackling the business of having the streets causeyed and pavements laid. Money always being short, whinstone setts were being laid at crossroads, with the intention of extending this work as money became available. Pavements were dealt with separately. Each householder was ordered to have paving flagstones laid along the street frontage to his property. Where no property owner could be traced, or at vacant sites the Commissioners would have ashes put down as a temporary measure. North Leith session was responsible for laying pavement along the churchyard wall in

Coburg Street, and this had so far been neglected. Presumably this was now attended to.

The reform of Parliament brought to Leith the novelty of the hustings. The early elections were totally unlike the quiet, staid scene at modern polling stations. Few Leithers were then entitled to vote, but the hustings provided a great public entertainment, and an excuse for a good deal of horse-play and rumbustious behaviour. At the first election in 1832 the Sheriff applied for the use of North Leith Church as a polling station. The kirk session asked for more information as to just what was required, but gave it as their unanimous opinion that 'The House of Prayer is not a fit place for political discussions'. At that time a polling station was something of which no one in North Leith had any experience. The Member of Parliament elected then was John Murray, who became Lord Advocate, and at the next election in 1834 he, with Adam White, the provost of Leith, approached Mr Buchanan the minister with the request that the portico of the church might be granted for use as a polling station. This time the session agreed, provided that 'there is to be no political discussion during the polling of voters'.

At this period there was no congregational roll, or roll of communicants but in 1834 a directive came from the General Assembly that such a roll should be kept. At the March meeting of session the moderator produced an alphabetical list of communicants known to him. This, at least, was something to build on. It was decided that as the minister had not been able to provide addresses with the names he listed, an intimation should be made in April, that everyone who came on the Saturday before communion to collect his communion tokens, should bring a slip of paper with his address on it, and the names of all communicants in his house. Mr Gillespie, the elder in charge of the token distribution, was told to see to it that facilities were available for any who came without the needful information, to write it down and hand it in. So the first communion roll, with much labour, was put together; but the result was less than satisfactory. The process had to

be repeated before each successive communion. By 1835 the
session had a list of 246 male heads of families, plus sixteen
elders. From this the total number of communicants can only
be guessed; it may have amounted to 600 or 700.

While this effort at organizing the membership of the
congregation was in hand, the congregation was rocked by a
highly embarrassing and sensational happening. The session
clerk, Thomas Scotland, had a maid-servant who gave birth
to an illegitimate child, and named him as the father. Mr
Scotland strenuously denied the charge, and an action raised
against him in the civil courts failed. The girl left Leith, but
the slur remained. The congregation was both embarrassed
and divided over the matter. The presbytery took the case up
and decided that a verdict of 'not guilty' in the civil court was
no bar to ecclesiastical investigation, and it was suggested that
only by swearing the Oath of Purgation could Mr Scotland
clear his character. Accordingly on 12 April 1836 the
moderator read the following letter to the session:

> Revd Sir   In reference to the decision of the presbytery
> of Edinburgh in the case concerning me, I beg you will
> administer to me the oath of purgation at your earliest
> convenience, in such a way as may be applicable to the
> case.
>
> (signed) Tho. Scotland.

The session then appointed two of its members to confer with
Mr Scotland and ascertain he understood the seriousness of
the oath. Scotland was then summoned to a special meeting
of the session and the oath administered and sworn. 'Where-
upon the Session resolved to assoilzie him from the charge
and to restore him to Church privileges.' He then resumed his
duties as session clerk and schoolmaster. A century and a half
later such a charge would be shocking: in the 1830s it cut
much more deeply, and it is pleasant to know that in the end
the session clerk's good name was not damaged.

Six months after Tom Scotland's reinstatement a new

church was opened and dedicated at Newhaven. This fulfil-
ment of a long-running project took place on Sunday 30
October 1836. For many years, probably since the death of
Dr Johnston, a mid-week service had been held in the
Newhaven school for the benefit of the aged and infirm who
found the walk to the parish kirk beyond their strength. It
had proved a popular innovation, not only for the elderly, but
also for younger folk, who found it convenient, they said, to
attend a local service mid-week rather than a Sunday service
in Leith. But it was well-known to everyone in the parish that
the Newhaveners always considered themselves as a separate
community, and greatly preferred worshipping together.

It was said that the idea of a church for Newhaven had its
birth at one of those mid-week services, when Mr Buchanan
arrived to find the schoolroom packed, and a number of the
elderly standing, unable to find any seats. The minister
recognized a problem requiring a solution without delay. At
the end of the service he said he was naturally pleased at the
large attendance, but pointed out that the elderly ought all to
have had seats before anyone else, since the service had been
started for their benefit. But it was obvious that Newhaven
wanted a church for the village, and a building fund was
started there and then, with a donation of £100 from Mr
Buchanan himself.

Services in the Newhaven Church continued to be conducted by ministers from North Leith for the next fifteen
months, until the appointment of the Rev James Fairbairn as
first minister of Newhaven in January 1838. Fairbairn soon
proved to be a gifted man with a flair for leadership. With the
bulk of his congregation however, he left the Established
Church at the Disruption in May 1843, and these dissidents
built St Andrew's Church at the harbour, where Mr Fairbairn
continued as minister, and was remembered with affection and
respect in Newhaven and North Leith long after his death.
When Mr Fairbairn was first appointed to Newhaven, the
North Leith session submitted to the presbytery proposals for
bounds to the new parish:

It is the opinion of this Session that the Road from the east end of Annfield crossing the Whale Brae and Cherry Bank and proceeding westward through Trinity to the boundary of the parish beyond Bellfield, is a natural and proper boundary between North Leith parish and the proposed new parish for Newhaven, and all residing to North of this line should be included in the said new Parish.

Sabbath schools were now proliferating, and several elders had schools organized in their districts. The chief difficulty was to find places in which to conduct these schools, where attendances averaged forty pupils. The parish schoolroom was used, but in other districts a school could only operate in a large room in a private house. A report on Sabbath schools in June 1838 ended with:

REMARKS—The School in Mr Schultz's district is now given up, the Teachers having lost the room on Mr Bairnsfather leaving the house. They have done all in their power, with the assistance of the Elder, to procure another suitable place in the district, or the neighbourhood, but are sorry to state that their endeavours have been unsuccessful. They still continue on the outlook and will report what has been done next quarterly report.

Despite difficulties, enthusiasm for the Sabbath school movement continued, and every now and again a new school would be opened in some untapped area of the parish. At the end of 1838 a class for servants was started on Sunday evenings, when presumably servants had an hour or two to themselves. This activity was taken up in the spirit of mission. The parish was no longer a community in which everyone knew everyone else. There was growing concern over the increasing number of those in the parish showing no interest in religion. Mr Buchanan was an ardent admirer of Dr Chalmers, the leader of the Evangelical party in the Church. Chalmers came to

North Leith in the autumn of 1838, and his preaching left a strong impression on the minds of the kirk session. It was decided to take action:

> There being some hundreds of North Leith parishioners who make no profession of religion and attend no place of worship; and as Mr Gall has at present no district in the parish, and is willing to undertake the duty; it is proposed to move that he be appointed, with the assistance of the parochial assistant and missionary, to follow up Dr. Chalmers' recommendation made to us in North Leith Church a few weeks ago, to use his exertions in 'excavating' those individuals and to endeavour to bring them back again to Churchgoing habits.

No more is recorded of this venture, and while Mr Gall was an enthusiast, it must be supposed that the distractions and excitement in Church affairs during the next few years prevented any sustained missionary work being continued.

A variety of concerns exercised the minds of North Leith parishioners in 1839. After long discussion it was decided to introduce gas lighting to the church. Gas pipes had gradually been laid in the streets since the mid-twenties, and the new illumination was a great advance on the feeble glow of the oil lamps. As yet few private houses had gas laid on, but people were at least aware of what gas could do in providing light. The elders thought the church lighting was inadequate and expensive, since only the finest wax candles were considered appropriate, and these were not cheap. So gas was brought into the church, and paid for by voluntary subscription—the well-tried and effective way to get things done that were seen to be desirable.

Leith's newly acquired independence brought with it many problems of local government. For the first five years of its existence Leith town council had no income, and during those years the town was financed by loans from private individuals. By the time the City Agreement Act was obtained in 1838 the town council was deeply in debt, and sought by every means in its power to raise money. This is probably why the magistrates allowed horse-racing to be re-established on Leith Sands in 1836, despite universal outrage expressed by all the Leith churches and by every other society able to make its objection heard. Petitions were addressed to the magistrates year after year without success, as the rental charged for the use of the Sands was too valuable to be abandoned. North Leith in 1839 had another matter for protest:

> The Session considering that they hold property in the neighbourhood of the Citadel, and that various Shows and petty Theatres have been erected in the vacant area by permission from the Magistrates, which was justly complained of as a great nuisance, authorize the Clerk to sign in their name any petition that may be drawn up and presented to the Court of Justiciary or other authorities, with the view of removing the nuisance and preventing a recurrence of the like in future.

But again, the rental of the ground for Shows and a Penny Gaff in the Citadel area was a welcome contribution to the municipal coffers. Incidentally the above extract from session minutes was from a meeting on Christmas Eve 1839. Christmas was not then recognized by the Presbyterian Church: it was a festival peculiar to Episcopalians and others. But although not included in the Church's calendar it was celebrated in a mild way in the homes of the people, and the kirk session organized and encouraged the distribution of free coal to the poor, and cheap oatmeal. It was a season for kindly feelings and generous behaviour towards those in need, leading up to the New Year family celebrations.

The same Christmas Eve meeting also considered another matter which had long been a source of irritation to the session. This was what was described as 'the desecration of the Lord's Day by Sabbath funerals'. The session 'cordially disapproved of the too general custom' of Sabbath funerals.

And they were not alone: all the churches in the town and all the ministers disapproved of the custom. Describing these funerals as a desecration of the Lord's day might seem to the twentieth century rather far-fetched, but the religious element in funerals then was slight, the general sentiment being that the deceased was past praying for since he or she was now in the hands of God. Moreover, at a time when death was so frequent a visitor, not too much attention was given to private grief, which was something to be accepted as an unavoidable part of life in this world. The desecration of the Lord's day lay in the heavy drinking that took place on those occasions, and the frequent consequence of argument and horse-play. The people preferred Sunday for a funeral, as that was the only work-free day in the week. Sabbath funerals continued despite clerical disapproval.

One Monday in August 1840 the kirk session heard from Mr Buchanan that he had received a presentation to the High Kirk (St Giles) in Edinburgh, and had accepted it, as he felt unable to cope with his present charge at North Leith as adequately as he would wish. Accordingly he would be inducted to the High Kirk on Thursday first. In other words the kirk session was told that in three days' time they would be without a minister! There had been no disagreement with Mr Buchanan, no complaints or ill-feeling of any kind. He was indeed a highly respected man, a strong adherent of the Evangelical party in the Church, which professed great dissatisfaction with the workings of patronage in the Kirk. Yet here was a prime example of one effect of patronage. Ministers could be presented to a charge without consulting the wishes of any congregation, although the Courts of the Church could approve or disapprove. James Buchanan's attachment to the Evangelicals apparently counted for nothing when he was offered the presentation to the High Kirk.

In that same year the new church of St Thomas was opened for worship in Leith. This was the gift of John Gladstone, an old North Leither, son of Thomas Gladstones the corn merchant, kirk treasurer and close friend of Dr Johnston.

Born on the Coalhill, John had betaken himself to Liverpool where he had made a fortune. Returning to Scotland he bought the estate of Fasque in Kincardineshire, where he spent the summer months, spending the winter months at 11 Atholl Crescent in Edinburgh. The story of the erection of St Thomas' Church began with the death of Mrs Gladstone in 1835, after a long period as an invalid. John then conceived the idea of having a hospital built for women with incurable diseases. He investigated the area around his birthplace on the Coalhill of Leith, and decided to build not only the hospital or asylum, but two schools for boys and girls, together with a church and manse. He had already built churches in Liverpool, and had become very friendly with Dr Chalmers, who held up John Gladstone as an example of Christian philanthropy.

In February 1839 the presbytery of Edinburgh received a petition with John Gladstone's proposals for building a new church at Sheriff Brae in Leith, with a manse, two schools, houses for schoolmaster and schoolmistress, all to be in connection with and under the superintendence of the Establishment. This lay on the table for a month, and in March a constitution for the proposed new church was produced. The ministers of South and North Leith, with the heritors and kirk sessions were warned to appear the next month for their interest. The constitution of the new church was approved by the presbytery except for a clause reserving the right of patronage in the church to John Gladstone, his heirs and assignees. Mr Gladstone (he became Sir John in 1846) was very angry at this objection to his patronage, but the Ten Years' Conflict which ended in the Disruption, was largely concerned with patronage in the Kirk. Dr Chalmers, Gladstone's erstwhile friend, was leader of the Evangelical wing of the Church, determined to bring an end to patronage, and he refused to support Gladstone's petition. The Assembly however, in May 1839, approved the constitution for St Thomas', including Gladstone's right of patronage. It was April 1845 before the presbytery agreed the bounds of the new parish, which were described as being those portions of the parishes of South Leith and North Leith:

> included within a line drawn from a point in Tolbooth Wynd opposite Riddle's Close, down the middle of the former street to the centre of the Upper Drawbridge, thence along the harbour and Water of Leith to the point where the Greenside Burn falls into that river. Thence along the line of the said burn to the Bonnington Road at Swanfield, thence to the foot of the said road, thence along Cables Wynd to Giles Street, to a point opposite Back of Vaults, thence along Back of Vaults to St Andrew Street and thence along Riddle's Close to the point in Tolbooth Wynd from which it set out.

When Mr Buchanan intimated his resignation he had indicated to the session that he had been influenced in his decision by the belief that he felt unable to fulfil all the duties of the charge in a satisfactory way. The session found this less than convincing, but if it were true that the duties connected with the incumbency had indeed grown beyond the capacity of one man to fulfil, perhaps North Leith ought to be made a double charge. A proposal to this effect was examined, but the elders decided against it. During the twelve years of Mr Buchanan's incumbency a number of important developments and changes had taken place in the parish. Newhaven had become a separate parish, with its own minister, and a further reduction of North Leith parish took place in 1839, when in May of that year the foundation stone of the Mariners' Church was laid. This was the culmination of almost twenty years of missionary work by the Edinburgh and Leith Seaman's Friend Society. The Society had acquired an old naval hulk from Greenock which was brought to Leith and berthed in the Queen's Dock (later known as the West Old Dock), free of all dock dues. Sunday services were conducted on board for seamen, who were invited to attend in their working clothes, as no one but seamen would be present. Before long Sunday and weekday schools for both children and adults were being conducted on the hulk. This 'Floating Chapel' was set up in 1821, and there was then no intention of the work there developing into a parish. The opening service was conducted by the Rev Andrew Lothian, himself an ex-seaman who said he rejoiced that 'this aquatic Bethel was prepared and opened, not by any sect, or for the little purposes of any party, but by those of every name, rank and condition who, from the great motives of humanity, religion, morality and patriotism, are Seamen's Friends'.

A young missionary was appointed, and John Thomson made a great success of the work. He became so identified with the Seamen's Mission that the hulk became known to all in Leith as 'Floating Johnnie's Kirk'. But the years took their toll of the old ship; the timbers rotted and there was no money for repairs. The Admiralty, who had given the hulk to the Society in 1820 refused to do anything more in the matter, and when it appeared that this valuable work was like to be abandoned for lack of accommodation, a proposal was made in presbytery at the beginning of 1839, that a church ought to be built for the work among seamen. With astonishing speed this idea was agreed and put into effect. Within four months of the original proposal the foundation stone of the new kirk was laid, and the General Assembly of 1839 approved a constitution for it. The presbytery of Edinburgh then considered the District and Charge to be assigned to the minister of the Mariners' Church, as it was already being called.

I The locality, or what in ordinary cases is the Parish, shall be Leith Docks and Harbour.

II The objects of pastoral superintendence, or what corresponds to the inhabitants of the Parish shall be 1st, the men who are employed on board the Vessels trading to and from the Leith Docks and Harbour. 2nd (on the ground that family ranks with the Head) the families of which such men are the heads, who reside in Leith, & 3rd, the Widows and families of such. This will give a population in port or on shore of about 1800 or 2000 . . .

The presbytery approved of this, but with the addition that the church itself, and the schoolrooms connected with it, were to be included in the District and Charge assigned to the minister of the said church. 'Floating Johnnie' was ordained and inducted to the Mariners' Kirk on 30 April 1840 at 12 noon. The Mariners' Kirk, like Newhaven and St Thomas' Kirks, took away a section of North Leith parish, and the population in the immediate vicinity of the new church were attracted to the service there. The North Leith elders reckoned that these three new churches now established in the original parish of North Leith had reduced the pastoral responsibility of the North Leith minister by almost one half during the twelve years during which Mr Buchanan had been minister.

Apart from that, the proposal to pay stipend to two ministers from the same income as had been required to pay one, was hardly realistic. What kind of minister would be attracted to North Leith with the promise of a pittance as stipend? There was also doubt as to the legality of dividing the stipend and the manse rent between two ministers without starting a costly process in the Court of Teinds. More than any other consideration however, the kirk session saw the need to attract an able leader, with a powerful and attractive pulpit presence. Despite the division of the parish in recent years, attendances at their kirk had in no way diminished, and this they attributed to Mr Buchanan's powerful and deeply impressive discourses:

> We therefore are greatly concerned in obtaining the ministrations of some highly gifted preacher, that thereby the present numerous and respectable congregation may be restrained from occasional wandering and perhaps ultimate dispersion.

It was soon evident that filling the vacancy was not going to be a straightforward quest to find a suitable minister and offer him a presentation. The Church of Scotland was deeply divided over patronage, and adherents of the two parties in

the dispute divided not only congregations, but even families
and friends. John Thorburn, son of David Thorburn, minister
of the second charge in South Leith at that time, recalled those
days from his boyhood:

> Party feeling ran so high that the old happy relations of
> families were wrecked, and as children we wondered why
> so many people were not on speaking terms with each
> other, who had been old friends.

This division now appeared in North Leith. The heritors,
elders and male heads of families whose business it was to find
a new minister, brought to the presbytery not one, but two
presentations in February 1841—one in favour of the Rev
Alexander Davidson, minister of North Esk Church, Inveresk,
and another in favour of the Rev John Macnaughtan of the
High Church, Paisley. The presbytery did what presbyteries
are prone to do when confronted with a problem: the question
was referred to a committee to consider and report. The kirk
session became alarmed at this. They had vivid memories of
the long litigation that had accompanied the move from the
old kirk to their present building, and of the horrendous
expenses involved. They urgently pled with both parties in the
congregation to sink their differences and accept whatever
judgement the church courts might offer.

Unfortunately the church courts came to no clear
conclusion. The matter was referred to the Procurator, and to
other Counsel, and both these learned gentlemen advised that
the presentation in favour of Mr Davidson was null, as there
had been irregularity in the way the oaths of the Patrons had
been taken. On the other hand, there were aspects of Mr
Macnaughtan's presentation that were not clear, and his
presentation ought to be recommitted. That was in May. In
June an appeal against the presbytery's judgement was lodged
from North Leith. The matter lay on the table until
September, when the presbytery clerk received a letter from
legal agents acting for the supporters of Mr Davidson,

saying they had been instructed to resist any move the presbytery might make to proceed on the presentation to Mr Macnaughtan. At the same time a petition was received from the supporters of Mr Macnaughtan urging the presbytery to proceed and sustain their presentation. The presbytery reaffirmed their rejection of Mr Davidson, but delayed action on Mr Macnaughtan.

The parish had now been vacant for over a year, and in the autumn of 1841, on presbytery advice, a temporary missionary or locum tenens was engaged for three months. In the event he had to be re-engaged more than once. Both parties continued actively in support of their candidate, but apart from his congregational responsibilities, the session clerk was busily engaged making the returns that were required at that time for the 1841 census. A new list of elders' districts was also compiled in June of that year. As the bounds of St Thomas' parish were not yet agreed, North Leith still counted a district on Coalhill and Old Bridge End, amounting to 108 families. Obviously an elder's district in the 1840s was a much larger responsibility than in the late twentieth century. In the main parish area there were fifteen districts averaging around ninety families in each. Another five districts were described in Newhaven.

In July 1842 Mr Hamilton Pyper, Advocate for the Patrons of North Leith who were presenting Mr Davidson, compeared before the presbytery and laid on the table a Declaration by the Court of Session stating that Mr Davidson 'is duly and effectually presented to the Church and Parish of North Leith'. He also produced the presentation itself. The presbytery hummed and hawed for some months, but finally rejected Mr Davidson's case in November, despite a strong plea by counsel in favour of that minister. On the presbytery's rejection of the case, counsel appealed to the Synod. The presbytery's judgement may not have been unaffected by a report it had just received from North Leith kirk session concerning a Call in favour of Mr Davidson. Of the signatures attached to the Call, the kirk session objected to 252, as being people who had no right to sign. This left 204 names, of which 130 were females. Of the 74 males signatures left, 35 had signed by mandate, although they themselves were resident in the parish. This left only 39 males who had personally signed. In addition to these objections practically all the female signatures were supplied by mandate. Mr Davidson's case would appear to have been irretrievably lost.

This was the state of North Leith parish and congregation at the beginning of the fateful year of 1843. Mr Macnaughtan of the High Church, Paisley, was now the unanimous choice of North Leith heritors, kirk session and male heads of families to fill the vacancy there. On a wave of relief and new confidence North Leith looked forward to filling the vacancy quickly. But when the congregation of the High Church, Paisley, heard of the proposed translation of their minister, they protested loud and long; moreover Mr Macnaughtan himself, perhaps having heard something of the divided state of the North Leith congregation, expressed no desire to leave Paisley. The matter was discussed by Paisley presbytery, was referred to the Synod of Glasgow and Ayr, and ended at the General Assembly, who pronounced a decision in favour of his remaining at Paisley. That was the same Assembly which saw the Disruption, which split the national Kirk, while North Leith still waited for a minister to fill the vacancy there.

CHAPTER 6

The Last Years of Patronage

The Disruption left the Established Church in disarray. Congregations all over the country were split as the dissidents left to form what was at first called the Free Presbyterian Church. The fortunes of this new secession have been recorded in great detail, but the story of the remaining Establishment has had nothing like the same attention. Those who 'went out'—especially the dissenting ministers—were saints and heroes: those who remained were taken to have neither principle nor conscience—determined to stick to their stipends and benefices, come what may. The popular jingle of those days summed up widespread opinion:

> The wee kirk, the Free Kirk,
> The kirk withoot a steeple:
> The Auld Kirk, the cauld kirk,
> The kirk withoot the people.

But the facts of the situation were different from that simplistic view.

North Leith was vacant at the Disruption, and more than half the kirk session—nine elders—left to join the Free Church, along with what was probably a similar percentage of the congregation. The split in the national Church had been brought about by the working of the Patronage Act, and the entrustment of ministers to charges where they were not welcome had forced the division of the Kirk. No minister had been forced on North Leith, where the patronage rested with the 'hail inhabitants', which in effect had come to mean the male heads of families. But what had been a fairly simple way of bringing in a minister to a village community, had changed into something much more difficult to handle and organize in a growing industrial town. It was much more difficult to get a consensus among hundreds of patrons than among a few dozen men. Each vacancy since the death of Dr Johnston had highlighted the difficulty of checking the credentials of each signatory. All through the present vacancy the congregation had been divided, backing rival presentations to Mr Davidson and Mr Macnaughtan. Mr Macnaughtan had eventually been ruled out, as he was unwilling to leave Paisley; but the Davidson party had appealed to the Synod against Edinburgh presbytery's rejection of their presentation as being irregular. The Synod of Lothian and Tweeddale referred this appeal to the General Assembly, but with the Disruption having upset the Assembly's business the 'North Leith case' came before the Assembly of the depleted Established Church a week later.

Mr Penney, advocate for Mr Davidson, set the facts before the Assembly. There was no denying that a large majority of the congregation had from the first favoured Mr Davidson as their minister, but the Macnaughtan faction had maintained the presentation to Mr Davidson was invalid, as the oaths of allegiance to the Government had been administered in front of only one JP instead of two. A lengthy spell of litigation had followed, at the end of which the Court of Session had dismissed the objection and declared the presentation valid. Macnaughtan's party had then made various objections to presbytery. Mr Davidson, they claimed, did not have the qualifications needed in a minister for North Leith. If Davidson were to be settled at North Leith the congregation would be divided and would remain divided. The 'greater good of the Church' would not be served if Mr Davidson were translated to North Leith. On hearing these 'dissents without reasons' Edinburgh presbytery 'without giving a deliverance on the relevancy and truth of the objections against the presentee' resolved to refuse to sustain the call, and refused to take any further steps in the settlement of Mr Davidson at North Leith. The General Assembly, to its credit, remitted the matter back to the Presbytery of Edinburgh, with instructions to 'proceed with the settlement with all convenient speed'.

A month later, on Thursday 22 June 1843, the induction took place at midday, before a congregation estimated at about 700. Obviously a great effort was made to do justice to what was seen to be an outstanding occasion in the congregation's history, and a triumph for justice and fair dealing. There is no way of knowing whether the Macnaughtan party had left the congregation for the Free Church, but there is no doubt of the warmth and sincerity of the welcome given to Mr Davidson, who was 'cordially welcomed by numbers of his parishioners as they retired from the church' after the induction. And in the evening of that same day almost 200 sat down to the Induction Dinner at the Royal Exchange building in Constitution Street. This was reported in the Edinburgh press:

> The highest testimonials were borne to the talents, usefulness and personal worth of the new minister; and there seemed to be but one feeling of satisfaction and delight, that a case which for so long had deprived the parishioners of North Leith of the regular administration of a settled pastor, had been so happily and harmoniously concluded.

The new minister could have been under no illusions about the state of the congregation and its future prospects. The numbers attending the induction and the enthusiasm there exhibited did not reflect the real situation in the congregation. The vacancy had attracted wide attention throughout the presbytery, and many visitors came to the induction. The members of the congregation were eager to show support for the new man, but there were not very many of them. There were only four elders left—Messrs Galloway, Malcolm, Goalen and Forrest; and only Galloway and Forrest were active. On the other hand the Disruption had tended to polarise attitudes in the parish: the dramatic exodus of ministers from the Establishment attracted many lukewarm members to go with them, but at the same time a kind of backlash within the remaining Establishment resulted in forty-four first communicants coming forward at the October communion. Two active elders were hardly sufficient to serve even the greatly reduced congregation, so immediately after the autumn communion male communicants were asked to hand in lists of men they would propose for the eldership. There was no lack of suggestions, for from those lists a leet of twelve names was drawn up, and it was agreed that if they were agreeable all twelve men should be elected. In the event only six men accepted and were elected. In February 1844, with eight active elders, the parish was divided afresh into eight districts, with an elder appointed to each.

Alex Davidson, aged thirty-eight, was at the peak of his energy and enthusiasm, but he had to cope with much bitterness and intransigence between denominations. In charitable work there was great need and plenty scope for co-operation with other churches in the parish, but this was not to be. Before the Disruption there had been a Clothing Society organized and operated by members of the congregation, but most of those involved in this work had joined the Free Church and would have nothing to do with their former friends and fellow-members. Mr Davidson proposed to form a new Clothing Society to be operated jointly by churches in the parish, but there was no response to the suggestion, although there was great need for the work. Dire poverty was widespread, but the Clothing Society was not just an agency for distributing cast-off clothes. The Society was funded by the wealthier members of the congregation who employed women to make clothes which were sold cheaply to the poor, and good second-hand clothes were cleaned and repaired. Perhaps after all the parish would be better off with two clothing societies. Another regular charity in winter was the distribution of free coal to the poor. In January 1845 it occurred to the minister that this work could be done more efficiently if all the congregations in the parish were to combine their efforts in one organization for this purpose. There were now five congregations in the vicinity. Apart from the parish kirk there was the Free Kirk, the Free Church in Newhaven, the Burgher Church which since 1820 had been the United Secession Church, and the Mariners' Kirk. These were each invited to join with the parish church in operating the delivery of free coal, but none would agree to take part. Posterity can only look with wonder on such small-minded jealousy showing within the Christian Church.

Newhaven was a problem. The minister, James Fairbairn, with the large majority of the congregation, had seceded at the Disruption, leaving just a small group faithful to the Establishment. As there were too few of them to support a minister they reverted to their former status as members of North Leith, and their church at Newhaven remained empty and unused for the next six years. The Newhaveners however regarded their situation as no more than a temporary set-back. They bided their time and gradually recruited new members until, in August 1849 a presbytery committee decided it was time to begin regular worship at Newhaven again. The keys of the church were handed to Mr Davidson, with instructions to have the church cleaned, and a precentor and officiating elders appointed in time for the next Sunday, when Dr Macfarlane of Duddingston would conduct the service. In the following October communion was celebrated in Newhaven Established Church for the first time since the Disruption. Forty-seven communicants attended, and by the end of the year almost 150 seats had been taken. The Home Mission Committee of the Church gave permission for the appointment of a missionary at Newhaven until a minister could be called, and the committee gave £50.00 towards the missionary's salary. On 18 April 1850 the Rev William Graham, from Wallacetown Church in Ayr, was inducted as minister of Newhaven, and there he remained for the next thirty-seven years until his death.

The rebirth of the congregation at Newhaven took place in an atmosphere of goodwill and co-operation, but the times were hard. The Irish potato famine in 1845 and the two following years brought an influx of Irish labour to Leith, where land was being reclaimed to build the Victoria Dock. But in 1846 the potato blight spread through much of the west of Scotland, and poverty and scarcity of food was general. On 21 March 1847 the kirk session was told:

> Wednesday first, 24th, is to be a Day of Fasting and Humiliation throughout the nation, because of the great scarcity and dearth of provisions. As the Presbytery has ordered the same services on that day as on an ordinary Sunday, it is agreed to take church-door offerings to raise money to buy provisions for the poor of the congregation.

There was as yet no congregational Sunday school. In Newhaven there had been a Sabbath evening school, but as the teachers had all gone into the Free Church, the school was now a Free Kirk activity in the village. Some time before the Disruption John Stewart Begg, a fisherman, had bequeathed a sum of money, the interest from which was to be used to support the Sabbath evening school. In August 1848 the kirk session received a request from the Newhaven Free Church Sunday School for payment of the interest of the Begg Bequest, which they had not received since the Disruption. The elders took the view that the bequest had been made to the Sabbath school conducted by the Established Church, but since the remnant of the Establishment in Newhaven had not had any Sabbath school since the Disruption, they agreed to pay over the outstanding interest, on condition of receiving a report on the way the money was spent, and reserving the right to make a fresh decision on the matter in future.

With a minister once more in charge at Newhaven, North Leith kirk session met there in June 1850 and ordained elders to serve that congregation. This presumably drained the parish kirk of suitable prospective elders, because when, three months later, seven were proposed for the eldership, they all declined. One of these was Sir John Watson Gordon the well-known artist, a long-standing member of the congregation, and a neighbour of Mr Davidson's at Catherine Bank on Newhaven Road.

Poverty was rife and drink was cheap, and the churches, so jealous of their denominational status, so suspicious of one another, were at least united on one thing. They all subscribed to a petition to the magistrates in April 1851 to cut down the number of public house licences, and to grant no new licence, in view of the prevalence of drunkenness in the town.

The ecclesiastical situation at Newhaven was one of intense rivalry. The Free Kirk there saw the re-opening of the Established Church as a challenge. James Fairbairn, the Free Kirk minister, with a reputation in that congregation as a devoted and well-loved pastor, allowed his kirk session in 1851 to issue circulars in the village claiming that the Established Church there could dispense no proper sacrament—that there was neither valid baptism, nor communion, nor valid marriage; that the members of the Established Kirk sat twenty-five Sabbaths in the half-year in the Newhaven church, and on the twenty-sixth they took communion in the parish kirk. As it happened, the circular was out of date by the time it was issued, as the kirk session of the parish church had just ordained elders at Newhaven, and the sacraments could be dispensed there, albeit by the minister of the parish kirk.

William Graham, presently settled as the Established minister at Newhaven, soon made his presence felt. He was fully as aggressive as his neighbours in the Free Kirk, and decided to press for the endowment of his church as a sure way to establish it on a firm basis. He took the Free Kirk circular to North Leith kirk session and proposed that the parish church should contribute to the endowment fund he was setting up. He acknowledged the good work the North

Leith session had done in having the Newhaven church re-opened, and suggested they should now donate to the endowment fund a proportion of their congregational income commensurate with the number of North Leith members who had 'relieved' the parish church by joining the kirk at Newhaven. If North Leith did not respond to this proposal, Mr Graham said he would turn to the Endowment Committee of the General Assembly. Not surprisingly the North Leith elders ignored this bizarre approach, but his was their first encounter with a man who was to prove a thorn in their flesh in years to come.

Since 1815, when the war with France ended, Leith had known almost unrelieved depression but, after the mid-century, shipping and trade generally entered a time of comparative prosperity. The new Victoria Dock was crowded, as were the Old Docks and the Harbour. Sail was giving way to steam, slowly but inevitably, and the old wooden-walled ships were being out-dated with the arrival of iron-hulled vessels. There was plenty of work in the shipyards, though poorly paid, and the population was growing as was the congregation. The old weeknight instruction of the congregation in singing had now borne fruit in a 'Band' as the choir was called, which regularly occupied its own pew, for which seat rent had to be paid. Mr Davidson had proved to be a great success in nurturing the congregation, decimated by the Disruption. He was now ministering to a vigorous fellowship of committed Christians. Evidence of this strength and confidence emerged at a meeting of the heritors and kirk session, when it was agreed:

> that the Kirk Session should undertake to pay the salary of the schoolmaster, the salaries of the precentor, the beadle and door-keepers, the expence of heating and cleaning the church, and the charges of Synod and Presbytery Clerks, on the understanding that they receive certain feu duties of the annual value of about £25, and all the collections made at the church door.

The Crimean War ran its course with just one brief mention in the session records, when a Day of Humiliation and Fasting was announced in March 1855 at the end of that terrible winter in which all the armies participating lost far more men by disease and starvation than by the bullets of the enemy. Locally a far greater stir was caused by the arrest of Robert Philip, Provost of Leith, on a charge of child abuse. He was a member of the North Leith congregation, and the kirk session suspended him from Church privileges, the main effect of which was to forbid him to take communion. He was later restored. Philip was a wealthy man who had well served Leith on the town council for many years, but his trial and prison sentence destroyed his standing in Leith and he left the town.

The Rev Alexander Davidson died on 5 April 1858, and the usual arrangements for such an event were made. The seats of the manse pew and of the kirk session were draped in black, and the elders all appeared in full mourning for three successive Sundays. A few days after the funeral, however, Mr Scotland, the session clerk, who was also the parish schoolmaster, called an informal meeting of elders in the schoolhouse. It had become known through the parish that William Graham, the Newhaven minister, was canvassing for votes, with the object of securing for himself the presentation to the charge of North Leith. Some said he had begun canvassing while Mr Davidson was on his death-bed. This was highly improper, and it was agreed to issue placards advising the patrons not to pledge their vote to anyone at this early stage. A vacancy committee had not yet been appointed; it was little more than a week since Mr Davidson had died, and Mr Graham's activities were in the worst possible taste—apart from the fact that the Newhaven minister was reputedly devoted to his own congregation.

Three days later the normal procedure for filling the vacancy was begun, when a public meeting of all the patrons was held. The following week, at the close of the Thursday evening service, the elders met to discuss what could be done about Mr Graham, who was vigorously pursuing his canvass:

It was suggested that Mr Graham may not be aware of the sentiments entertained of him by the whole of the Elders, and, in so far as they can judge, by a large majority of the congregation, and in these circumstances the Elders deem it to be their duty both to the Parish and to Mr Graham, to communicate with him before he proceeds further in his canvass.

A deputation interviewed Graham, whose response was evasive and unsatisfactory. Most people in North Leith saw him as a bumptious, conceited and aggressive man for whom they had neither respect nor toleration. Mr Graham, a man still in his thirties, nevertheless belonged to the old school of thought—to the Moderates, who had for long formed the backbone of the Establishment. To their way of thinking, what a congregation thought of the minister was neither here nor there; the important thing was to secure the presentation, and once the minister was settled in the charge it was up to him so to care for his people that they would grow to understand and appreciate him, like him and even love him. The Disruption had been a revolt against the way of thinking. What Mr Graham failed to understand was that since the Disruption there had come about a considerable change in many Established congregations, who expected to have much more to say in the choice of a minister than in the old days. And in North Leith, where the patronage was shared among the whole congregation, filling the vacancy was a matter of general interest. On the other hand the Newhaven minister knew that his congregation consisted almost entirely of North Leith members who lived in and around Newhaven. He knew that he was highly thought of in Newhaven, so if he could depend on their votes, that gave him a considerable advantage in any competition for the presentation. Newhaven was not yet a parish, but merely a mission or chapel-of-ease attached to North Leith, so Newhaven votes would certainly count towards the presentation decision.

At the public meeting of patrons a committee was formed

to attend to the business of filling the vacancy, and a sub-committee was given the task of finding a sole nominee who might be recommended to the patrons. The sub-committee learned that a petition was being prepared by Mr Graham's supporters to have him nominated for the vacancy, so they very quickly approached a well-known minister they had had in mind—the Rev William Smith of Trinity College Church in Edinburgh—a congregation then without a home since the old Trinity College Church was demolished in 1848 to make way for the Waverley Station. In Mr Smith's time the congregation had worshipped in the Waterloo Rooms, and later in Canongate Free Church, rented for the purpose. At first reluctant, Mr Smith was eventually persuaded to allow his name to go forward. The sub-committee then made their recommendation, which the kirk session unanimously supported, and the patrons warmly welcomed the proposal to have Mr Smith presented to the vacant charge.

At that point Mr Graham shocked everyone by raising an action for interdict at the Court of Session. All proceedings in the vacancy were then sisted, and a long period of waiting ensued until the case came forward. The Rev Archibald Buchanan, minister of St Thomas' Church, was appointed interim moderator, and he presided over a session meeting in January 1859 when it was decided to defend the action. This would inevitably be a very expensive business were Mr Graham to succeed in his petition, so the elders hastened to assure Mr Smith he would be put to no expense in the matter—a necessary assurance, as the session were nervously aware that Mr Smith might wish to withdraw from the field to save expense, and to avoid the mounting ill-feeling the case would provoke.

All through the summer and autumn of 1858 the congregation of the parish kirk had discussed the coming case endlessly, as no one had any inkling of the grounds on which Mr Graham could raise his action. When at last the matter came to court it transpired that what was at issue was the true interpretation of the Act of 1606, by which the patronage of the living was vested in the 'haill inhabitants' of the parish. Mr Graham was well aware that when Mr Davidson had been presented to North Leith in 1843 many of the signatories to the presentation had not been legally entitled to sign, and that no action had been taken then to rectify the situation since it was obvious that the great majority of the congregation wished Mr Davidson for their minister. Graham was now petitioning to have the legality of each signature examined. Counsel for the defence pointed out that the action was incompetent. Instead of challenging Mr Smith as the rightful presentee, Mr Graham ought to have challenged each signatory as a party to the action, and until this was done the action could proceed no further. Counsel for the pursuer answered that if that were to be done something like 1800 persons would have to be individually cited; but in fact that would be ridiculous, and in several other similar cases it had been deemed sufficient for one candidate in a presentation to raise an action against his competitors. Lord Neaves, the Lord Ordinary, agreed, and suggested that if the defender wished to make 1800 citations he should do the work himself—at his own expense.

In the event Lord Neaves' interlocutor appointed a scrutiny of the votes for each candidate to be made to determine the legality of the voting. Now just at this time—on 20 July 1859—the Court of Teinds met and decided to erect Newhaven Church to the status of a parish church *quoad sacra*, with an endowment of £120 towards the stipend, and £11.1.4 to pay feu duty and repairs annually. This enhanced Mr Graham's standing. He had lodged a reclaiming note against Lord Neaves' judgment, and this allowed him to take further action in the case if he wished, but for the time being he let the matter rest while he examined the implications of what might be called his promotion to be parish minister of Newhaven. Towards the end of 1859 he took North Leith kirk session to task over baptisms and the publication of banns. He rightly pointed out that when these affected Newhaven people—members of his congregation—the North

Leith session must not interfere, as they had been doing by continuing to baptize and proclaim the banns of Newhaveners. This was an oversight by the North Leith session—understandable perhaps during a vacancy, when the minister responsible was the interim moderator who was scarcely *au fait* with the intricacies of North Leith parish and the new status of Newhaven Kirk. While Mr Graham certainly scored a point here, he never seems to have realized the depth of feeling against him in the parish. The following month, January 1860, he was again in communication with the North Leith session. This time he made it known that he was willing to abandon his claim to be minister of North Leith, provided the kirk session paid him 100 guineas towards meeting his legal costs! This effrontery elicited some rancour among the elders, but they were now well enough acquainted with Mr Graham to realise he could continue to cause trouble for a long time. They were also deeply concerned that the parish had now been vacant for almost three years through Mr Graham's activities, and that the congregation was suffering in many ways. They accepted the compromise offered, paid the money asked for, and with great relief turned to other business.

There was a time when North Leithers were rather proud of the system of patronage used in their parish. That the right to present a minister to the charge was vested in the 'haill inhabitants' instead of the landed proprietors in the parish, was a reason for quiet satisfaction. But times had changed; the nature of the community had changed; and since the death of Dr Johnston each vacancy in the parish had produced more trouble and difficulty when the antiquated system was again put into operation. The General Assembly of 1844 had passed an Act providing for objections to ministers presented to vacant charges, and no distinctions of sex were made in the Act. This, whether deliberately or by oversight, gave women in the Church of Scotland the right to vote. As we have seen, women in North Leith signed the presentation to Mr Davidson in 1843, and this was challenged at the time. The

1844 Act made it possible for women to sign the presentation to William Smith, and they must have been counted among the 712 who signed that call.

Within a month of settling with Mr Graham the kirk session were approached by their lawyers, Messrs Mann & Duncan, suggesting that the elders should sign a petition to be forwarded to the Lord Advocate, who was, by coincidence MP for the Leith District of Burghs in the Reformed Parliament, asking that the patronage system in North Leith be changed. Patronage had been giving trouble in many parishes. The attention of the General Assembly had been called to several instances where the rights of patronage had been sold to the highest bidder during a vacancy. In 1858 the Assembly had instructed the Lord Advocate to prepare a Bill for Parliament to deal with this and other anomalies in the exercise of patronage in the Established Church of Scotland. Most of the session signed the petition readily, but two— Messrs Webster and Thomson, dissented, as they felt it would be unfair to deprive the heritors of their right of patronage, since 'they not only built the church, but have to keep it in repair, pay manse rent, and other burdens'.

All outstanding problems and worries, doubts and fears were set aside and forgotten for the time being as the 15 of March 1860 approached—the day on which the vacancy, the three-year vacancy at North Leith, was filled by the induction of the Rev William Smith to the charge. At the time the congregation simply celebrated the arrival of a new minister in their midst; but when the young people of 1860 were able to look back in old age, they could see that date, that event, as a milestone in the history of the congregation. From that day North Leith parish church, after seventeen years of anxiety, frustration and infighting between parties, entered on a long sustained period of vigorous growth and prosperity.

Mr Smith, aged forty-one, was already well-known in the Established Church. All over the country *quoad sacra* parishes were being set up as the population of the older parishes increased. This had happened at Newhaven within the old parish of North Leith. Each of these new parishes had to be endowed for a minimum of £120, and it was reckoned that a capital sum of £3000 would produce that amount of annual income. It was with this nationwide endowment of *quoad sacra* parishes in view that the Assembly of 1846 appointed an Endowment Committee under the convenership of Professor Robertson. While he was at Trinity College Church William Smith became deputy to Professor Robertson on the committee, and on Robertson's death in 1860 Mr Smith became convener. By that time 200 parishes had been endowed, with a capital sum of £600,000, and for the rest of his life the work of the Endowment Committee occupied a large part of William Smith's time—a laborious, time-consuming work and responsibility.

The mid-nineteenth century was a period of many changes in society. Sometimes the session was active in trying to effect what they saw as desirable change, as in curtailing the number of public house licences. Another long-continued effort by all the churches and the newly formed Temperance Society to get rid of horse-racing on the Sands was eventually successful in 1859, when the last of these races were held. By contrast the elders were somewhat perturbed at the rapid increase in the Roman Catholic population in Leith, mostly among the labouring class arriving from Ireland. In 1848 an unknown benefactor had enabled them to acquire Balmerino House, with its garden, in the Kirkgate, where they proceeded to build themselves a church. Two years later Dr Wiseman was appointed Cardinal Archbishop of Westminster, and it was proposed to divide the country into papal dioceses. The session protested to the Crown, but realized this could be no more than a gesture. It was more immediately disturbing, following the introduction of compulsory registration of Births, Marriages and Deaths in 1855, that a Bill came before Parliament to direct parish records to be handed over to the Registrar General. North Leith session registered their objection. Before long however, the session became closely involved with the new registration system. The schoolmaster's house at 40 Bridge Street was being extensively repaired just as Mr Smith arrived as the new minister. When work on the house was completed it was rented to the town clerk for use as a Registrar's office for North Leith, while the schoolmaster, who was also session clerk, presumably continued in the house he had occupied while the repairs to his old house were being carried out.

At that period members of the Established Church had no experience of contributing to the Schemes of the Church, or to the maintenance of the ministry. The work of the Assembly's Endowment Committee went on against that background. Church door collections had traditionally gone to the poor of the parish, but since the introduction of the Poor Law and assessments for the poor many people simply gave nothing to the Church. Income for the kirk session came from seat rents, and rents and feu duty from any property in their possession. After Mr Smith arrived a list of liabilities was presented at a session meeting:

Schoolmaster's salary	£21.–.–
Session Clerk's salary	5.–.–
Precentor's salary	30.–.–
Beadle's salary (15s per week)	39.–.–
Church cleaners	5.16.–
Male Door Keepers (2)	4.–.–
Stove attendance	2.8.–
Coals	4.5.–
Expenses at sacraments	23.–.–

Beadle's salary to be raised to £1 per week, he finding his own house. Session Clerk applied for an increase—to be considered.

In an industrial town like Leith there was no escaping the poor, or avoiding the problem they presented. Especially in winter, when hundreds inevitably lost weeks of work through bad weather, poverty in many homes became destitution.

Before William Smith's arrival a Home Mission Agency had been at work in the town. A number of people had clubbed together to pay a divinity student £70.00 a year to work as missionary throughout both North and South Leith. He visited the destitute, doing what he could for them, and he conducted services both on Sundays and weekdays at Hillhousefield, at North Leith Poorhouse and at Back o' Vaults in South Leith. This work was undenominational. Financial support came from members of various churches, but the working committee was mainly composed of North Leith members. Mr Smith judged this work to be too thinly spread over too wide an area. One divinity student in his spare time could not cope with the clamant need off the whole town. He therefore instituted a Parochial Association which undertook the same home mission work within the parish of North Leith. Services at Back o' Vaults were discontinued, and instead Sunday meetings were held on the Coalhill. For two years the Parochial Association continued to support the student, but thereafter the work was carried on by members of the congregation of North Leith. It was a remarkable advance, which appears to have been the first parochial experiment in mission work in the town. It was taken up by other congregations, until in the next generation every church in Leith had its own mission.

The abject povery of so many Leithers had lain on the conscience of the Church for a long time, but no one knew the answer, and it was widely assumed to be one of the facts of life in this world, as Jesus had indicated in the Gospel— 'The poor ye have always with you'. The Rev William Mackenzie was minister of North Leith Free Church in 1856 when he proposed to build a 'Church for the Poor' on land he hoped to acquire in St Andrew Street in South Leith—the site of the old Laigh Market. This was a complicated business, as various former proprietors among the former trade incorporations still had an interest in the site. Just at that time a colleague was appointed to work with Mr Mackenzie at the Free Church, and he took the opportunity to pay a visit to

Australia. On the way home he died and his body was buried at sea.

The twentieth century Church would recoil from the idea of a Church for the Poor. It would seem to polarise Church membership, emphasising the difference between the 'haves' and 'have-nots'; but the idea was conceived in the environment of the mid-nineteenth century, when society was structured rather differently from what it was to become in the next century and a half. The poverty of those days has long passed away in this country. The threadbare poor could not appear in church without embarrassment to themselves and to the bien members who paid seat rent. But William Mackenzie's idea of a church to be built for the poor was too grandiose, even had he got the site, and the money to erect the church. William Smith made use of accommodation already being used at Hillhousefield, the Poor-house and the Coalhill, where elders had their district Sunday schools. These mission services were completely informal, held in bare rooms with wooden benches, and worshippers dressed as well as they could manage, knowing they were on an equal footing with everyone else present. In time these meetings developed a fellowship and an ethos of their own. They were conducted by all kinds of visitors, many of them divinity students. Unlike the normal congregational worship, the speaker, be he minister, student, or visitor, was not important; what mattered was the fellowship, the knowledge that one was not alone in poverty, sickness or suffering. The missions also provided focal points for ladies in the parish church to make contact with the poor. In mid-Victorian times, better-off people were socially completely isolated from the poor, and the two groups lived in ignorance of each other's way of life. The ladies provided tea and buns at the mission services, became acquainted with the regular attenders, realized some of their outstanding needs, produced cast-off clothing for the needy, and organized soup kitchens in winter. Some genuine friendships were formed in this way. Congregational missions pioneered social welfare work. They amounted to a small drop in a vast ocean of need; but seed was sown in these early meetings that in time would yield a great harvest in social welfare. William Smith was in at the start.

He also developed the Sunday school idea by introducing to his parish a congregational Sunday school. These Sabbath schools, begun more than half a century previously as a means of getting neglected children off the streets, were now to be developed along institutional lines, providing religious education for the children of the congregation. Started in 1862, the parish Sunday school rapidly grew, and with an enthusiastic and committed staff, the number of children attending posed a considerable problem in accommodation.

Reverting to the petition sent by the kirk session to the Lord Advocate during the vacancy in 1858, this bore fruit in:

An Act to abolish the Annuity Tax in Edinburgh and Montrose, and to make Provision in regard to the Stipends of the Ministers in that City and Burgh, and also to make Provision for the Patronage of the Church of North Leith (23rd July 1860) 23rd & 24th Victoria cap. 50 sect. 31.

This Act provided that:

... The right of Patronage or of the Presentation of a Person to be Minister of the church and parish of North Leith, heretofore belonging to and exercised by the 'hail inhabitants thereof' under the Statute 1606 chap. 27 or by any of them shall, from and after the passing of this Act, Cease to be in and belong to the said 'hail inhabitants', and the same is hereby transferred to and vested in the male persons being of full age, whose names shall appear in the Valuation Roll in force for the time as proprietors or occupiers of any lands and heritages situated within the said Parish of North Leith, hereinafter termed 'the heritors', and the whole male Communicants whose names shall stand in the Communion Roll of the said Church and the Congregation thereof; and within two months after the passing of this Act the Heritors and Male Communicants shall meet on such day as shall be named by the Kirk Session, of which meeting intimation shall be made from the Pulpit of the said Church and also by Advertisement in three or four Newspapers published in Edinburgh not less than eight days previous to such meeting . . . and by a plurality of voices the meeting shall nominate a Committee of their number, not exceeding twenty-five, of whom a majority shall be a quorum, and the Committee shall forthwith proceed to frame Regulations as to the time and manner of calling and holding future meetings of the Heritors and Communicants, and of voting thereat . . . &c . . . and the Regulations so made shall forthwith be published by Advertisement . . . and shall after such publication be submitted for the approval of the Sheriff of Midlothian, and when approved by him shall be valid and effectual, and the whole future procedure shall be regulated thereby; and when any election of a Person to be a Minister shall have been made under said Regulations, it shall be sufficient that the Deed of Presentation be subscribed by the Chairman of the Meeting at which the Election shall be made, and by any three Members authorised by the Meeting to subscribe same along with him . . . &c . . . &c.

This Act took away the patronage from the 'hail Inhabitants' and vested it in the heritors and male communicants, and two years later Mr Smith urged the kirk session to decide on how long a man might absent himself from communion before being disqualified from exercising his right as a patron. Patronage in North Leith had become unworkable, and this Act provided not for its abolition, but for its transformation into a system that could be monitored and controlled. Up to a point this was satisfactory, and certainly an improvement on the old arrangement, but right through the country there was a groundswell of opinion against the continuation of patronage in the Established Church. In April 1866 an overture for the abolition of patronage was approved by the presbytery of Edinburgh, and when this came before the General Assembly the next month William Smith spoke strongly in its support. It took several years of debate and consultation to bring patronage to an end, and Mr Smith (who became Dr Smith in 1869) was actively and deeply involved in the negotiations, as the trusted adviser of both churchmen and politicians. Patronage had been the rock of offence when the Disruption split the Church, and there is little doubt that the abolition of that system gave the worthy Doctor hope that the two sides in the Church might soon come together again. This in fact did happen, but not until Dr Smith and the generation after him had passed on their way.

In the obituaries published after his death Dr Smith was described by more than one writer as a traditionalist, thirled to old ways and slow to accept change. This is quite misleading; the minister had a strong sense of the value of traditional ways and customs, and indeed was not willing to change without good cause. At the same time all were agreed that the North Leith minister was a very able business man who made a notable success of the Church's Endowment Scheme, for which he worked long and hard, apart from his duties as parish minister. The fact is that this genial, sociable man was a glutton for work, hating inefficiency and waste. The long-drawn-out communion services irritated him, and within a year from his settlement at North Leith he had the communion tables enlarged. The old system of dispensing the elements still prevailed. There was no permanent communion table. When the sacrament was to be dispensed, tables were brought in to a space cleared in front of the pulpit, and for long and weary service after service, the congregation were served in turn round these tables. By enlarging the tables more people could be served at one time, and the overall length of the exercises on Communion Sunday was shortened. The idea caught on: a year or two later the Rev James Mitchell in South Leith Church followed suit, and this continued until the modern method was introduced a generation later. The following year saw the appearance of communion cards to take the place of the old communion tokens. This was certainly an advanced idea in the 1860s, but by the end of the century cards were in general use.

Seat rent was then a main source of income for the Church, and in the autumn of 1862 an interesting arrangement was agreed by the kirk session. It had been suggested that the choir, or band, as it was indifferently known, should be accommodated in a raised pew. The manse pew appeared to be the most suitable for the purpose, and the minister agreed to move his family to accommodate the choir. As all the pews were already rented, it was a problem to know just where to put the manse family. However, there was a front pew in the south gallery, shared by Mr John Mitchell of Trinity, and the Dock Commission, and this was acquired by the session for the minister's family at a rent of six shillings sterling per bottom room per annum. Also, in front of the new raised pew there were two pews which no one was likely to want, as those sitting there would have the choir immediately behind them. These pews were taken over by the kirk session, one at 25/- and the other at 42/- a year, for the use of the poor. In view of what has already been said concerning the poor and the Church, it is not surprising that these two pews should have been thought sufficient for that purpose.

The General Assembly in 1864 decided it had no objections to *Hymns for Public Worship* being introduced to congregations. Hitherto congregational singing had been confined to the Psalms. In October that year Mr Smith produced several copies of the new hymn-book to the session, assuring the elders that these verses were linked to many fine tunes. North Leith probably had no small opinion of the music in their worship, with the choir prominently seated in a raised pew. The session after taking three weeks to think it over, resolved unanimously to introduce the new books to the congregation.

Since the sale of Dr Johnston's manse in 1825, North Leith Parish had had no manse. The ministers found accommodation where they could, receiving an addition to their stipend in lieu. This was unsatisfactory both to the kirk session and the ministers, but a suitable manse was hard to find, as South Leith had discovered earlier in the century. This need was supplied in 1866, when the house known as Leith Mount, which had been occupied by the minister for the past year, was purchased by the heritors for £1850 to serve as a manse. There is some mystery and confusion here however. About the year 1850 North Leith UP congregation purchased the house called Leith Mount—'a substantial and commodious house'—for their minister, Dr Harper, 'and Leith Mount continued to be his family house, and to be associated in Leith with his familiar and honoured name, for the next thirty years.' So says Principal Harper's biographer. The confusion here has probably arisen from later generations applying the name Leith Mount to a house (or houses), whereas originally the name applied to the site—roughly defined by Ferry Road, North Junction Street, Prince Regent Street and Madeira Street. Whether that is the explanation or not, in the second half of last century these two houses were each known as Leith Mount. Both have now been demolished.

Our Victorian ancestors were odd people in some respects. They were punctilious about dress and appearance, with rigid rules in regard to mourning, and suitable dress for elders, for whom a morning coat with a white necktie was *de rigueur* at communion and other special services; yet the behaviour of the congregation left a lot to be desired. More than once Dr Smith had to rebuke his people for their unseemly habit of hurrying to the door immediately the benediction had been pronounced. They were urged to sit down for a minute or two before making for the exit, but as this injunction had to be repeated it looks as though the old habit died hard. At this period there was a movement among a small group of members, to introduce new ways of worship, encouraged perhaps by the changes Dr Lee had been introducing at the Greyfriars Kirk in Edinburgh. The choir, from its elevated position, was beginning to sing anthems, and the congregation, which until recently had sung only the metrical psalms, was not only being encouraged to sing the new hymns, but was also being led by the choir in chanting prose psalms. In March 1868 one elder had the temerity to move in the session that 'it be resolved with the view of further improving the service that the congregation be recommended to kneel during prayers and stand during singing'. This proposal failed, but it showed the forward-looking views of some members.

Most of the congregation did not share these advanced views, and it was then that the egregious Jacob Primmer appeared on the scene. He was a divinity student, a member of North Leith and a teacher in the Sabbath school. He had a fixation about the Roman Catholic Church, and all through his controversial career that passion never abated. According to his own account, he heard that there was a proposal on foot to introduce an organ to the church. He decided to organize opposition to this and other innovations. With two other members 500 signatures were obtained to a petition protesting against the chanting of prose psalms and the singing of anthems. He also wrote to the *Daily Review* against the introduction of instrumental music to church services; but his methods generated opposition as well as support within the congregation. A few weeks later, at the Sunday afternoon service, which was well attended, Primmer was refused entry to his pew by a burly cooper who was already sitting there. This large workman said he had been employed by one of the elders to keep Primmer out. They began struggling together, and the worshipper in the pew behind retrieved his silk hat which he had laid in Primmer's pew for safety. Jacob Primmer managed to sit down where the hat had been, and the cooper pinned him there. Still struggling, the cooper's foot slipped and he jabbed Primmer violently with his elbow. Primmer stood up and called out, 'I take you all as witnesses of the assault committed on me by this man'. At this point Dr Smith entered the pulpit, and that was the end of the disturbance. Later the cooper apologised, but Primmer took him to court in a civil action before the Sheriff. Many witnesses were called from the congregation, the assault was proven and the cooper fined five shillings. The importance of all this, from Primmer's point of view, was the publicity, and as he himself later commented, the result was an end to all innovations for many years.

The larger communion tables no doubt helped to shorten the overall length of public worship on Communion Sundays, but apart from that the half-yearly sacramental seasons in April and October conformed to the traditional pattern. The celebration began on Thursday Fast Day, when there were services forenoon, afternoon and evening. The Saturday service followed, when the tokens, now cards at North Leith, were handed out. Sunday worship continued all day till late afternoon, and then a service in the evening brought that exhausting day to a close. Finally there was a Monday thanksgiving service. For all this several ministers were required—generally about six. A typical programme for a sacramental season was arranged for the April communion in 1868:

Thursday 23rd April
           Forenoon   Revd John M. Lang,
                           Anderston Church Glasgow.
           Afternoon Revd James Macnair M.A.
                           Auchtermuchty.
            Evening   Revds Smith, Lang & Macnair.
Saturday 25th .   .   .   Revd Alexander Thomson Cosens,
                           Broughton
Sabbath 26th .   .   .   Revd Wm Smith, Minister of the Parish.
                           Revd Archd Scott, Maxwell Church
                           Glasgow.
                           Revd Willm Bennie, Kelvinhaugh
                           Glasgow.
                           Revd Alexander T. Cosens, Broughton.
Sabbath Evening . .   Revd Archd Scott, Maxwell Church
                           Glasgow.
Monday 27th .   .   .   Revd Thomas Gordon, Newbattle.

The visiting ministers were all given hospitality at the manse. John Lang from Anderston, Glasgow, and James Macnair from Auchtermuchty stayed overnight on Thursday, and on the Saturday night Mrs Smith would be obliged to cater for Messrs Cosens, Scott and Bennie, and these three would not depart till Monday. The twice-yearly sacrament was therefore a very busy time domestically, apart from the religious exercises of that long weekend.

This was gey auld-farrant even in mid-Victorian times, and was attracting diminishing support. In October 1869 the Saturday service was dropped, together with the Thursday evening service; and by then the Fast Day was becoming a holiday for the general public. On a fine day in the last week in April members of the church would attend the Fast Day service in the forenoon, and in the afternoon go for a sail over to Burntisland, or up river to Stirling, or join an afternoon excursion to the country. The next generation would see the Fast Days disappear.

Dr Smith's death was widely and deeply lamented. At the age of fifty-seven he had worn himself out. Through his work as Convener of the Endowment Committee of the Church over many years he was known throughout the country. Since he took over the convenership in 1860 he had seen no fewer than 192 parishes added to the Church of Scotland, each of them endowed. Between them, Professor Robertson and Dr Smith had built up an endowment fund of about £1,700,000— an immense sum for those days.

His irenical spirit attracted many friends from all denominations. He was happy to associate with and preach in the churches of those who usually had little to do with each other. The Free Church, the United Presbyterian, the Baptist and Independent churches, Dr Smith saw as brethren in Christ, and at a time when even within the Church of Scotland there were wide differences in theological thought, and too often bitter party spirit, Dr Smith had the knack of bringing a mixed company to a state of mutual regard and good feeling, even if only for the time being.

His funeral was a great local occasion, widely reported and commented on in several obituaries. Some impression of that memorable day may be had from the

ORDER TO BE OBSERVED AT THE FUNERAL
of the late Rev. Wm. Smith D.D.
Minister of North Leith.
Saturday 17th February 1877.

1 Midlothian Coast Artillery Volunteers.
2 Provost, Magistrates and Town Council of Leith.
3 Ministers of other Denominations.
4 Endowment Committee of the Church of Scotland.
5 Leith School Board.
6 Presbytery of Edinburgh.
7 Kirk Session of North Leith.
8 THE HEARSE.
9 Relatives.
10 Congregation.
11 General Public.
12 Private Carriages.

Company to walk six abreast

CHAPTER 7

Towards Union and Unity

When Dr Smith died the parish was rapidly changing. The industrialized area around the church and the Citadel was still commonly referred to as the town of North Leith, and the village of Newhaven and the hamlets of Bonnington, Hillhousefield and Damhead were still separated by open country given over to farming, nurseries and market gardens. The irregular parish bounds followed the Water of Leith from its mouth to Bonnington Mills; then north-northwest to the Anchorfield Burn; then along the course of that burn to Inverleith; then due north to the shore of the firth at Wardie. This area, when Dr Smith took over, had about 11,000 inhabitants, and this figure had increased at an almost constant rate of 400 per annum since then, till in 1877 there were almost 16,000 people within the bounds. This increase had to be accommodated, and such was the demand for building sites that land values were rising steadily and the rural aspect was changing. In the Trinity area large villas in their own grounds were appearing as building proceeded, while nearer the town end tenements and terraced housing were quickly covering all available ground.

This was therefore a parish of great potential—potential which to a remarkable degree was being realised under Dr Smith's ministry. A man of energy, leadership and vision was needed to carry forward the work begun by Dr Smith. In the previous twenty years North Leith had emerged as one of the foremost congregations and parishes in the Established

Church; and to add to the air of excitement and anticipation, this was the first vacancy in the parish since the abolition of patronage. For the first time the congregation could select the minister of its choice without reference to any patrons. The congregational roll stood at almost 2400—a heavy work-load for any minister. A vacancy committee was appointed. That committtee was inexperienced, and perhaps somewhat naive. They had all been impressed by a young minister who had recently visited North Leith at a communion season—John McCulloch of Gourock, a young man of twenty-six. They invited him to take the charge of North Leith, but he had sense enough to decline, having, as he pointed out, only been two years in his present charge. Eventually the Rev Robert Stewart from Duns accepted the call, and came to Leith in October 1877.

Mr (later Dr) Stewart's ministry was short, for he was translated to Jedburgh in December 1881. His four-year ministry has been dismissed as of little account in the history of the congregation—a period when nothing remarkable happened or was achieved. This is quite mistaken. Many years later Lord Salvesen remembered Robert Stewart, under whom he had sat as a young man:

> In some respects he was a contrast to his predecessor (Dr Smith). His sermons were all carefully written and possessed a literary finish that is rarely lavished upon pulpit discourses. Few men that I have heard had such perfect elocution, and few indeed, could rival him in the lofty and earnest tone with which they were delivered.

That is an impressive assessment coming from such an eminent judge as Lord Salvesen. Lord Sands also thought very highly of Robert Stewart, rating him during his North Leith period as one of the coming men of the Church. But he considered Stewart's acceptance of the call to Jedburgh as a great mistake. And while Stewart later returned to Edinburgh as minister of New Greyfriars, he never became the influential leader in the Church his real abilities would have justified. The fact would appear to be that the physical strain of ministering to such a huge congregation as North Leith was too great. His departure for what was then the rural retreat of Jedburgh caused both astonishment and dismay in Leith. Certainly the kirk session had realised the great and inescapable demands on their minister, and from the time of Mr Stewart's appointment they had engaged an assistant, paying hims £120 a year. This was a help, but also an added responsibility, for assistants need guidance, advice and encouragement.

Robert Stewart's incumbency covered changes in the method and manner of public worship which marked the transition from long-established traditions to the modern style. In July 1878, less than a year after the new minister's induction, a proposal to introduce an organ to the church came before the kirk session. This apparently harmless contribution to the improvement of congregational singing was then regarded as a very serious matter. The use of instrumental music in church was a burning issue. Organs were indeed appearing in an increasing number of churches, but in every case there was strong opposition. North Leith followed the pattern exhibited elsewhere. A congregational meeting in November was attended by over 600, of whom 156 expressed uncompromising disapproval. After the meeting the argument continued outside in Madeira Street. Tempers frayed and the argument became a fight. The end came when about a dozen of those involved arrived at the police office in Charlotte Street, preferring charges against each other. But authority there seems to have pacified the belligerents—at least to the extent of dropping the charges. Despite the vociferous opposition the trend of opinion in the congregation was definitely in favour of the change, and in 1880 an organ with thirty-three stops was introduced at a cost of £750.

Once the idea of change had been accepted, one thing led to another. The plan for the organ brought out the need, or at least the desirability of a new pulpit, to be mounted in front of the organ. And while these developments were being worked on through the summer of 1880 the kirk session and heritors approached the well-known firm of architects, Messrs MacGibbon and Ross, to report on the state of the pews. Unless this was attended to the new organ and pulpit would offer an unfavourable contrast with the rest of the church interior.

The architects produced a scathing report. Twenty pews in the centre of the church before the pulpit were removable, and at each communion season they were replaced by 'Table seats' at which the communicants sat in turn. This meant a succession of at least seven Table services on Communion Sundays, 'and indeed we may say that during a considerable experience of such matters professionally in various parts of Scotland we have seen nothing of the kind more inadequate to requirements'. The rest of the pews were loose, shaky and extremely uncomfortable. They were disfigured with carved initials, they were unvarnished and extremely dirty. MacGibbon and Ross recommended that all the pews should be swept away and the church reseated, with no moveable pews, and all the accommodation being made available for communion purposes. What was being proposed, in fact, was the abandonment of the old style of communion service, in which the communicants in turn sat round tables to receive the elements, and the introduction of the method rapidly being adopted elsewhere, in which the elements were brought from the communion table to the communicants seated in the pews.

This was done accordingly, so that 1881, with the new organ and pulpit, and the new style of dispensing communion, was an unforgettable year in the congregation's worship. The new way of celebrating the sacrament made it necessary to have a considerable increase in communion vessels. Recognising this Mr Stewart, with the help of some friends, presented to the kirk session six salvers to be used in distributing the bread. This he did in October 1881, in time for the first dispensation of the elements under the new system. It was January 1885 before six communion cups were presented, again by the then minister and members of the congregation. These were exhilarating changes coming in quick succession, and the people may well have been wondering 'what next?' But the next change was a nasty jolt. The minister was leaving—and leaving the stimulus and busyness of a large town congregation for a parish almost at the back of beyond. At first they were incredulous, but they had to accept the fact that Robert Stewart had had enough, and was looking for respite.

The kirk session and congregation were thrown into confusion. Just when everything seemed to be set for a vigorous and inspiring future in North Leith, the congregation was suddenly leaderless. The elders lost no time. In less than four months from the start of the vacancy a successor to Mr Stewart was ordained and inducted, and that event was the talk, not only of Edinburgh, but of the whole country. To fill this charge of well over 2000 members the session had recommended, and the congregation had enthusiastically elected a young probationer, twenty-five years old, without any experience in charge of a congregation. It looked like a recipe for disaster.

Andrew Wallace Williamson was licensed by the presbytery of Edinburgh in the spring of 1881, and was appointed assistant to Mr Stewart of North Leith at the beginning of June. This in itself was considered remarkable, for assistants in a notable charge like North Leith were usually men who had served already as assistants in other charges. What was special about Williamson? Looking back from the end of the twentieth century it is not easy to realize the immense power and influence of public speaking a hundred years ago. With no radio, television or tabloid journalism, the public speaker attracted attention from all ranks of the community. That was the period of William Gladstone's Midlothian campaign, when hundreds turned out at every meeting to applaud, criticize, heckle and discuss what the Liberal leader had to say—and then to read verbatim accounts of the speeches in the newspapers next day. Ministers of the church were public speakers, and the sermon counted for much more than in modern times in assessing a Minister's ability. Andrew Wallace Williamson had no experience in managing and leading a congregation, but he could preach. There is no lack of witnesses to his surpassing ability in the pulpit. Preachers must be both born and made. Wallace Williamson, in an age when extempore preaching was greatly admired, prepared his material meticulously and wrote out his sermons carefully, as many ministers did: but when it came to delivery the true preacher's instinct came into play. He seemed both to create and to sense the atmosphere. From the moment he entered the pulpit there was a rapport with the congregation which built up until every worshipper was on the edge of his seat. Perspiration poured from him, yet he seldom raised his voice and he was sparing of gesture. Those who heard him agreed that his eyes had a strangely compelling light in them. The same had been said, a century before, of Robert Burns.

Even as Mr Stewart's assistant, Wallace Williamson's charisma had been felt by the whole congregation and his election to the charge appears to have been unanimous. He himself was taken aback. On Mr Stewart's departure he had assumed his assistantship might be terminated, and had already begun looking for another post. The ordination and induction took place on Thursday 13 April 1882, and the mid-day service was followed by the Ordination Dinner—a celebration which had long been associated with ordinations and inductions, and remained customary until the First World War.

The dinner took place in the Duke Street hall at 3 pm. This was the hall of South Leith parish church, erected in 1875, and the only place in Leith where a large company could be seated for dinner, apart from the Assembly Rooms. The organization of this function is of some interest now. The food and drink were supplied by the Commercial Hotel in Leith, and tickets were 7/6d each, this including a pint of wine between each two diners; any other wines or spirits to be paid for when ordering. The kirk session was responsible for cleaning the premises afterwards. Mr Phipps, a senior elder, took the chair, and three others acted as croupiers. All the ministers in the presbytery of Edinburgh were invited, and all the Protestant ministers of the town of Leith. Mr Andrew Grant, MP for the Leith District of Burghs attended, and the new minister was sent six tickets for his friends. The *Scotsman*, the *Edinburgh Courant*, the *Daily Review*, the *Leith Burghs Pilot* and the *Leith Herald* newspapers were all sent tickets, and the church officer was also given a free ticket. Almost one hundred sat down to dinner—all men, of course. Ladies did not attend these functions. The afternoon was enlivened with many toasts and many speeches, and in the evening at seven o'clock there was a congregational soiree in the church with 'a Service of Fruit which Messrs Hamilton and Lindsay have agreed to supply in bags at six pence each'. Tickets for this entertainment were priced at 9d, and throughout the evening several addresses were given and music provided by the choir and organist. Robes were presented to Mr Williamson and no doubt everyone went home happy.

The following week the minister took his place as moderator of the kirk session, and at once proposed that two assistants instead of one should be engaged. He had worked long enough with Mr Stewart to realize that in such a large congregation it was impossible to cope adequately with the day-to-day duties and responsibilities with only one assistant. That was the stressful situation that had led to Mr Stewart's early departure. If the session would pay the second assistant £120 a year, which was deemed appropriate for the first assistant, Mr Williamson himself would contribute £80 from his own stipend. This was agreed, and before long James Ray and Henry Farquhar were appointed to assist in the charge. These two were probationers—men in their twenties—a year or so younger than Andrew Williamson himself. The three young minsters hit it off together and were soon functioning as a very successful team. That year, 1882–3, was marked in the memory of the congregation as 'the reign of the boys', and there was a kind of euphoria attending the activities of both ministers and office-bearers, who all seemed to be of one mind, with any amount of energy and enthusiasm for the work—and, it should be added, many hilarious evenings at the manse when the three ministers met to report on their work and plan ahead. It was a situation quite unlike what the twentieth century has thought of as typical Victorian Church life. It didn't last. It was not expected to last, as the probationer assistants would soon be going to charges of their own. But the shocking thing was that the minister himself broke it up. Andrew Williamson remained at North Leith not much more than a year before going off to the second charge at St Cuthbert's. What was wrong with North Leith? This large congregation, so carefully nurtured and built up by Dr Smith, now seemed unable to attract and retain a minister.

There were many recriminations over Andrew Williamson's departure after so short a spell. The reason for this surprising move was never stated, although there was no end of discussion as to its wisdom, and speculation on possible deterioration of personal relationships in North Leith. One anonymous letter to the *Edinburgh Evening Courant*, however, put a finger on what was possibly the truth— especially as the allegation so publicly made in that letter was never denied. The rumour was that Andrew Williamson had become engaged to a young lady, of whom the upper middle-class coterie in the congregation did not approve. The reason for this was that the lady worked for her living. She was well-educated and talented, and was independent enough to disregard the prejudices of her time and class, and to be holding down a job at the *Scotsman* office. Andrew Williamson struck by her, realized the trouble in the congregation that might well follow his marriage with her, and so closed with the offer from St Cuthbert's, where the kirk session were apparently quite happy with the minister's intentions. A fortnight after his translation to St Cuthbert's Andrew married Agnes Blackstock. Whether in fact this was the real issue forcing a decision on the North Leith minister there is no recorded evidence to show, but it was widely discussed at the time, and it is worth noticing that after this brief stay with the congregation and abrupt departure, the North Leith elders and congregation never lost their affection and esteem for their brilliant young minster, and invited him back to Leith time and again, on suitable occasions.

Kirk sessions did not then normally advertise for a minister to fill a vacancy—they depended on personal contacts. At this juncture then, it was not surprising that the session should remember John McCulloch of Gourock, who had declined their invitation to him after Dr Smith's death. He had now been almost nine years in his present charge, so North Leith again approached him, and this time he agreed to come to the port, and was inducted on 11 March 1884. His arrival was hailed by the congregation with not a single dissentient, and at the age of thirty-three, energetic, experienced in pastoral work, and with a magnificent, flexible and resonant voice, he appeared well suited to the charge.

He found a Sunday school with almost 1000 scholars, which had to meet in the church at the close of the afternoon service. The infants—almost 250 of them—met in what was then known as the hall, the present session-house in Madeira Place. These restless youngsters were so cramped in that room, that some were seated on the ledge of a bookcase, and some on the mantelpiece! Rather belatedly thinking of safety, the session provided a fireguard, which afforded some relief to the teachers, who did not have their problems to seek. The older children meeting in the church were blamed for a good deal of horseplay and damage to property. They were allowed to come off the street through the iron gates into the church ground while the afternoon service was still in progress, as nothing could prevent many of them arriving well before their time, and scandalizing the neighbourhood by playing in the street on a Sunday. Having got into the church ground they then irritated the congregation by racing round the church walls and yelling to each other. When the kirk skailed the high-spirited scholars rushed in, pushing past the emerging worshippers, who complained to the kirk session. After several complaints the elders at the beginning of 1884 drew up a set of rules for the Sunday school children:

> Anyone climbing the railing or otherwise getting into the church grounds except by the gates shall be dismissed from the school. The Superintendent and Teachers must enjoin children not to injure or damage the Church hall or Session house, they shall not stand upon the seats or jump from one seat to another or otherwise do anything to damage pews.

But how effective could legislation be for 750 youngsters in those conditions? Sunday school was a wonderful, blessed interval of freedon and hilarity in the midst of a dreary, late-Victorian Sunday.

Many adults still thought that the ideal was that children should be seen and not heard. Sunday school teachers knew better, but most of these were themselves scarcely adult. Damage to the pews was particularly irritating, as this was the new seating only recently provided when the communion arrangements were changed under Mr Stewart. But while the children were too boisterous on occasion, some adults could be quite unreasonable. Mrs Neill of Lixmount complained to the session in June 1881 that her pew had been occupied (presumably in her absence) by Strangers! The session clerk was directed to reply regretting the inconvenience, and promising to put notices in the lobbies preventing a recurrence of any such thing. This was a job for deacons, but two months later the deacons reported that they had done their best, but could not think of any suitable form of words to meet the case! Not surprisingly. How could strangers or visitors be welcomed to the church but forbidden to sit in any pews for which seat rent had been paid? The session agreed to 'leave the matter over in the meantime'.

The need for a proper church hall had been discussed since 1881—a hall, in fact, to accommodate the Sunday School.

Obviously the Sunday school—especially a school as large as that in North Leith—was an institution of the greatest importance for the future of the church. South Leith parish had had to face the same problem a few years earlier, when their hall was erected in Duke Street. It was high time North Leith followed suit, and the new minister lost no time in pursuing the matter. Just two days after his induction Mr McCulloch brought before the kirk session the urgent need for adequate hall accommodation, and the meeting agreed unanimously. The minister thought the ground adjacent to the church would be suitable, and of course would eliminate the need to purchase a site. A committee was formed to investigate possible locations, but it made no report until November, by which time a great deal of investigation had been completed, and the report was full and detailed.

Fortunately the Baptists were having a church built in Madeira Street that summer, just about a hundred yards from the parish church. The contract for that building was £2400, and it was hoped the total cost would not exceed £2800. Guided by this the North Leith committee considered they could have a hall built for £3000, once a site had been obtained. The church ground was vetoed. A hall there would detract from the appearance of William Burn's building, and would almost inevitably darken the church. After considering the various options the committee recommended a vacant piece of ground between Allan Street and Great Wellington Street. They were informed this land might be had at £125 an acre, and as they would only need quarter of an acre they hoped to get a feu of £25 per annum. This ground was level, and was situated where a large increase in population was expected, for there were proposals to develop the area by extending the line of Allan Street and crossing it with another street running through Mr Salvesen's grounds. Ten years later this development took place with the building of the Dudley complex. The new halls would be within a stone's throw of Lapicide Place and Wilkie Place, which would be targeted for mission purposes, so the new buildings might qualify for a grant from the Church's Home Mission Committee, as well as from the Baird Trust. It was also suggested that morning services might be held in the hall simultaneously with the services in the parish church, and so relieve the pressure there, as there were far more applications for sittings than could possibly be provided. A worshipping body in the hall might then prove to be the most effective means of forming a second Established Church in the parish. Lastly, the proposed site was very near to the Tramway Car—the horse tram, that is: electric trams only arrived after the turn of the century.

All this made a case the session found most acceptable, so at a congregational meeting a month later Mr Edward Salvesen the advocate (later Lord Salvesen) moved the adoption of the proposal to build the halls at Great Wellington Street at a cost of £3000, and this was agreed. The foundation stone was laid on 12 January 1886 by Lord Balfour of Burleigh, and Prinicipal Cunningham opened the new halls on the 3 October following. It was claimed that 1000 people could be accommodated in the building, but the Victorians had no compunction about overcrowding. At the congregational soiree to mark the opening, over 600 attended.

The Thursday before Communion had for generations been observed as a Fast Day. This was the introduction to the communion season, and two services were held then, as on a Sunday. The Fast Day was a holiday from work so that people might attend church, but since the mid-nineteenth century the holiday aspect of the Fast Days had been obtruding more and more. Just as the new halls were opened, the kirk session received an enquiry from presbytery asking for their attitude to the Fast Day. For some years past in North Leith there had been no second service on the Thursday, as so few people were attending, but the morning service was still quite well supported, and it was on that occasion that new members were admitted to the Church. The session replied in these terms to the presbytery, but not long afterwards the Fast Days were abandoned, and these days became the spring and autumn holidays, transferred a few years later to the nearest

Monday, thus providing the novelty of holiday weekends. In their place the churches held preparatory services, usually on the Friday before communion. Ten years later, in 1897, there was a movement to change the second service on Sunday from the afternoon to the evening, and the congregation was asked to vote on the question. The result was 1227 in favour of a change to the evening, and 487 preferring to keep to the 2.30 pm service.

Evening worship was not entirely new even then. After Dr Smith's death an evening service was introduced for the months of June, July and August—no doubt to allow church people freedom to enjoy the summer Sunday afternoons outdoors, if they wished. In the winter of 1889–90 a series of five monthly evening services was organized, conducted by various eminent preachers. These were in addition to the two regular services, and were reasonably well supported. There seemed little doubt that most people preferred the evening to the afternoon for worship. Even so, attendance in the evening was never comparable with the morning congregation, and the First World War dealt the evening service a blow from which it never recovered.

The minister and office-bearers were far from satisfied with the Church's role in the community. Well aware of widespread poverty, and the poor wages earned by industrial workers, there seemed no way to affect such a transformation in society as would provide fair shares for all. They also recognized that despite the increasing size of the congregation there was in the town a hard core of indifference to religion which showed no sign of diminishing. At the same time the session felt bound to repeat the principles on which they had been brought up, even if some of these were beginning to be seen as prejudices and taboos, rather than principles. When the Young Men's Mutual Improvement Society connected with the congregation asked permission to have a dance after their annual meeting, their request was turned down immediately and unanimously. The church Literary Society sought permission to admit ladies to membership of the society, but that too was given short shrift, the session being unanimously of opinion that 'they do not think it expedient that such a change should be made.'

At the end of 1887 a questionnaire from the presbytery produced an interesting response from North Leith. The subject was non-churchgoing:

> *Question*: What do the kirk session regard as the chief causes of that alienation from the Church?
>
> *Answer*: Irregular employment and the consequent migratory life and poverty of a number in the parish. Intemperance, by poverty, arising in part from irregular employment, by migratory habits developed in a similar way; by the system of seat rents and family pews, limiting seats very much to those who own them, or can afford to pay for them, by the absence of aggressive measures on the part of the Church, such as services to which the non-churchgoing might be invited in their working-clothes: among other causes as affecting North Leith congregation, may be mentioned, change of minsters in recent years, and consequent vacancies, the size of the congregation and incompleteness in pastoral visitation, the frequency with which minsters have been, owing to calls made upon them elsewhere, absent from their own pulpit, tending to a want of continuous interest in the services and indifference on the part of the people.

At that time the population of the parish was reckoned as between 15,000 and 16,000. Membership of the congregation stood at 2766, of which about 1100 were parishioners.

Non-churchgoing was an issue worrying the General Assembly, and four years after the presbytery's questionnaire the Assembly's Committee on Christian Life and Work sent another list of questions:

If there be any form of secular work or employment usually occupying any persons in your parish on the Lord's Day, or during the preceding night, so as to prevent their due observance of that day, and to debar them from Public Worship, you are to give any information in your power.

The answers provided by the kirk session open a window for us on working life in North Leith in 1891:

I   *The Nature of the Occupation or Occupations*:

Policemen, Dock Gatemen and Piermen, Ships' Watchmen, Seamen, Dairymen, Stablemen, Cabmen, Domestic Servants, Shopkeepers in small shops retailing confections &c, Druggists, Crews on board pleasure steamers during the summer months.

II   *How much of the time on the Lord's day or preceding night is ordinarily occupied?*

Policemen, all day. Dock Gatemen and Piermen, during tide time. Ship's Watchmen, all day. Seamen, all day. Dairymen, all day. Stablemen, all day. Domestic Servants, not known. Cabmen, all day. Shopkeepers in small retail shops, all day. Druggists, part of the day. Crews of pleasure steamers, all day.

III   *Number of Persons so occupied during any one period.*

Policemen, 2 in street, 4 in docks. Dock Gatemen and Piermen, 6. Ships' Watchmen, 4. Seamen, about 250. Dairymen, 12. Stablemen, 6. Domestic Servants, not known. Cabdrivers, 2. Small shopkeepers, 15. Druggists, 5. Crews of pleasure steamers, 35.

IV   *What Proportion of Sundays of the Year may the same Persons be so engaged?*

Policemen, alternately. Dock Gatemen and Piermen, alternately. Ship's, Watchmen, constantly. Seamen, off and on

9 to 10 months. Dairymen, constant. Stablemen, alternately. Domestic Servants, alternately. Cabmen, constantly. Small shopkeepers, alternately. Druggists, alternately. Crews of pleasure steamers, constant for 5 months of the year.

V *Reasons assigned for the existence of such occupations*

No answer.

VI *Can you suggest any means by which such work might be restricted or dispensed with?*

No! Except by enforcing the Law that already exists, or amending it where it is defective, as to Sunday trading.

Non-churchgoing was certainly an unanswerable problem for those who saw the ideal society as one in which everyone was a regular church attender. Ministers and office-bearers realized that non-churchgoers, like the poor, would always be an element in society. What worried them was the increase in poverty and non-churchgoing. Other problems could be dealt with as circumstances and attitudes changed. One of these was the Fish Tithes which from the early seventeenth century had contributed to the stipend of the parish minister. There had always been opposition to these tithes, and the matter at last came to a head when the Dock Commission decided to promote a new Dock Bill in Parliament, in which one clause would provide for the ending of the Fish Tithes. The kirk session were petitioning Parliament against the Bill, but Dr Macarthur, a member of session, strongly opposed this, as he maintained it would certainly fail, would bring no benefit to the church, and would involve much expense. Mr McCulloch agreed with him and, no doubt after some private conversation, the Dock Commission invited representatives of the kirk session to a meeting. The outcome was that the Commission agreed to pay the session £2300 'as the commutation of the Fish Tithes exigible in Leith and

Newhaven.' And so, quietly and quickly, a centuries-old grievance was brought to an end.

The communion roll continued to increase. Every six months anything from forty to sixty new communicants were added to the roll, which by 1893 stood at over 3000. The idea of using the new halls as a basis for a second church in the parish was actively pursued with services at Great Wellington Street at 11 o'clock on Sunday mornings. In March 1893 Mr Philp moved at a session meeting:

> That the kirk session are of opinion that in view of the large and increasing population it is eminently desirable that a New Church be erected in the Bonnington district.

This was unanimously agreed. It was further agreed:

> That the session will gladly grant facilities by means of their Hall in Great Wellington Street for the formation of a Congregation while the church is being erected, so far as this can be done without hampering the congregation of North Leith in their use of the Hall.

Fourteen years earlier a similar proposal had been made with the intention of naming the proposed new church the Smith Memorial Church in memory of Dr Smith who had recently died. That scheme came to nothing, but in 1893 the matter was pursued more effectively, though still slowly. By 1900 a site had been decided on at Bonnington Brae, the kirk session had promised £800 toward the cost, and private subscriptions totalling almost £700 were also expected. The new church was erected in 1901, and the Rev Tom McCordindale took charge. The Bonnington Brae Chapel, as it was known, never attained parish status however. It was maintained as a chapel of ease of St Cuthbert's Church but was finally closed in 1924.

In the 1890s Mr McCulloch conducted a Band of Hope attended by some 600 children. This remarkable figure reflects the fact that with the large families then common the children in the parish must have numbered thousands, and apart from the Sunday school there was no organization in existence to interest and occupy youngsters. This state of affairs was changed when on 3 January 1894 the minister announced a proposal to start a 'Boys' Brigade' in the Hall, and calling for the co-operation of the kirk session. All the elders cordially approved of the proposal. It was novel. News of what had been happening in Glasgow under the inspiration and leadership of William Smith had reached the east of Scotland and this was the first move in Leith towards a similar experiment.

The idea had been discussed for some months, and an unsuccessful attempt to start a company before Mr McCulloch's formal announcement to the kirk session, and fresh plans were already well in hand. On 23 February 1894 the first meeting of the Company was held, and the first boys enrolled under the Captaincy of William Ferrier. But the Company, later known as the 1st Leith, made rather an uncertain start. No one had any personal experience of how to organize, plan and control the activities of a BB Company. The boys found it all exciting, thrilling and eagerly anticipated the BB night each week. Coping with their high spirits however, was a challenge, and made demands on time and energy beyond anything the officers could have anticipated. In the absence of any records from those early years we can only guess at what was happening. Perhaps there was a lack of support and interest from the kirk session and congregation. But people then could hardly know what kind of help was needed. There was no BB organization, no other local companies to compare with. The company drifted along while the officers gradually learned this new art of leading and inspiring boys. Their efforts achieved neither failure nor success, until in 1904 Alexander Lethem, a Leith merchant and member of the kirk session, took charge, and for the next twenty-four years the BB company was Alex Lethem's hobby, pride and joy. He made of it the biggest company in the port, and called for such standards of efficiency, commitment and enthusiasm in both officers and boys that old men in the late twentieth century still remember their boyhood in the 1st Leith as the greatest influence for good in their young lives outside their own families; and lifelong friendships were forged under A J Lethem's leadership. Mr Lethem never allowed the session or congregation to forget the BB company, constantly reporting on their activities and plans as opportunity offered.

The real reason for the difficult start of the BB company, however, may be found outside immediate church circles. The port of Leith in the 1890s was densely overpopulated, and had long been notorious for sanitary deficiencies. The Boys Brigade Company was started at a time when the directors of Leith Hospital had issued an ultimatum to the town council. For many years they had been urging the necessity for a hospital in Leith for infectious diseases, and the town council, year by year, had done nothing in the matter. Finally the directors, responding to the urgent protests of the hospital doctors, refused to accept any more infectious patients to be nursed under the same roof, and by the same staff as attended to the non-infectious patients. That ban came into effect on 1 October 1893, and in the following winter the port suffered a smallpox epidemic. A report of the Missions Committee of the kirk session reflects something of the general apprehension in the town:

> The Committee regrets that owing to the smallpox scare the (Church) Magazines were not for a few months delivered in some of the Districts with the accustomed regularity, and as, in the circumstances, the Ladies could hardly be expected to go willingly through the infected districts it was arranged to discontinue the issue of the Magazine for the two months of July and August.

There could hardly have been a worse time for the attempt to start a BB company. No boys could be recruited from infected districts, and the parents of boys in unaffected areas would be most reluctant to allow their sons to mix freely with other boys from fear of infection. The new company almost certainly was made up of boys from better-class homes in districts clear of the smallpox, and from families well known to each other. After the epidemic had passed it would be hard to bring in new recruits from the poorer areas of the town always under the threat of epidemics from insanitary conditions. Alex Lethem saved the little company from extinction, and by the strength and charm of his own personality brought new life to the company.

Nevertheless the work of the parish had to continue, despite epidemics or any other upsetting developments in public life; and indeed the winter of the smallpox saw a signficant quickening in congregational life. In the same month of January, when the proposal for a BB company was first put to the session, the first meeting of the Woman's Guild in the congregation took place. Once again it is difficult, almost a hundred years on, to realize the importance of what happened on the evening of 30 January 1894, when fifty women of the congregation gathered for the inaugural meeting of the Woman's Guild. In the century of its existence the Guild has flourished, and become so closely integrated with the life of the congregation that it would now be difficult to realize congregational life without the Guild. Long before the question of women in the eldership was debated, the Guild represented a power behind the scene, wielding considerable influence without having any official standing in the courts of the Church.

Mrs McCulloch, the minister's wife, was the first president, and she explained to the meeting the aims and objects of the Guild, and pointed out that this association would provide an opportunity for women to get together to discuss ideas and to get to know each other better. It was completely new: there had never been anything like it before in the lives of women in Scotland. The first two or three meetings heard addresses on the various activities of the congregation, and month and month the range of their interests extended. By the end of that first year 130 women attended a party—rather a staid party, their great-granddaughters might think—when they heard an address from the Deaconness and some vocal and instrumental music; and these delights were preceded by tea, cakes and fruit. The catering account for that evening has been preserved:

	£	s	d
120 fancy cakes at 1d..		10.	–
240 fancy cakes at ½d..		10.	–
Tea Scones		2.	–
2 Loaves			8
1½ lbs Tea		3.	–
Sugar		1.	–
Cream		2.	–
22 lbs Apples		5.	3
2 dozen Oranges		1.	–
6lbs Grapes		2.	6
Hire of 120 Cups and Saucers		3.	–
″ 120 Tea Spoons		3.	–
″ 2 Bread Plates			6
″ 6 Fruit Dishes			6
	£2	**4.**	**5**

True to form, the kirk session, aware of the many social problems confronting them, were determined to maintain the traditional attitudes of the Kirk—attitudes lingering from days when society was very different from what it had become. So no dancing was allowed in kirk premises, no ladies were admitted to men's societies; and in January 1895 an attempt by the Church Literary Society to hold a Burns Supper in a hotel was firmly vetoed. Knowing the session would never permit a Burns Supper in the Church hall, the Society had tried to evade Church discipline by arranging the event elsewhere, but it was no use.

That was a minor matter; there were larger issues to be resolved. The size of the congregation brought an immense burdern of pastoral work to the minister and his assistants, and it was only too clear to them that certain areas of pastoral concern could only be effectively covered by the ministrations of a woman. Mr McCulloch suggested that the session might consider employing a parish sister. They agreed, and at the beginning of December 1896 Miss Sophie Lamond was appointed 'to work among the poor of the parish' at a salary of £80 a year, half of this sum being provided by the Church of Scotland Women's Home Mission Association, and half by the kirk session. Miss Lamond remained at North Leith for two years, at the end of which she resigned, her health having broken down. The doctor was recommending her to pass the winter abroad. What 'working among the poor of the parish' meant, will be better understood in the light of a report made by Mrs Brown, the first district nurse employed by Leith Hospital. The work of the parish sister took her into the same type of housing described there:

> The enforcing of cleanliness is often a great difficulty, the obstacles being, the life-long habits of the people, the dilapidated condition of their houses, want of a sufficient supply of clothes and bedding, bad accommodation for washing and drying the clothes they have, and sometimes too little light to enable one to see whether things are clean or dirty.

In conditions like these the social worker, whether district nurse or parish sister, would require to be of robust health indeed to escape infection or the attention of vermin. Miss Lamond was succeeded by Miss Buchanan, who also remained two years and was followed by Miss Russell, who after rather less than two years had to be given two months' leave of absence to recover her health. It was a demanding job undertaken by a succession of women with unlimited compassion and devotion.

The turn of the century and the Edwardian era saw a number of changes in the church, each of which was important to the people involved, but all of which, three generations on, may be seen as no great matter, yet all of them marking steps in the Kirk's adaptation, materially and spiritually, to the unceasing changes in society. The Church Hymnary was introduced in 1899, to replace the *Hymns for Public Worship* of 1864. Hymns had increasingly won popular favour, especially since the visit of Dwight Moody and Ira Sankey, the American evangelists, to Leith in 1873. The Church Hymnary was unanimously welcomed by the session, and at once the organist and choir were provided with copies of the new hymn-book by an anonymous donor.

At the same period incandescent gas lighting had been on trial in the church, and had met with such approval that three lights were installed outside the church. But this was not good enough for some members, and a committee was appointed to investigate the possibility of bringing in the new electric lighting. No time was lost, and in 1900 the kirk session and heritors agreed to share the cost of installing electricity. The next year Christian Salvesen and his wife presented a communion table and chair. This was followed by the anonymous gift of a brass reading desk for the communion table, and Mr and Mrs McCulloch presented a font. Mr Salvesen then wrote a cheque for £1000 to benefit the poor of the parish; considering that a labourer earned less than £100 a year, and the sick and unemployed had no benefit at all, this was a splendid gift.

With some surprise we learn that as early as 1908 the General Assembly instituted an enquiry among congregations to discover the attitude of members to the introduction of individual communion cups. North Leith reported there was no general feeling in the parish in favour of any change in the manner of celebrating communion, although one or two individuals in the congregation had indicated their dislike of the common cup. The session concluded that if there should be an overwhelming body of opinion in the Church at large in favour of bringing in individual cups they would accept the inevitable, but that short of such a majority, those favouring individual cups might be served at a different time or on a different day. No more was heard of this until after the Great War.

John McCulloch's semi-jubilee as minister of North Leith was celebrated on Sunday 14 March 1909, when the morning service was conducted by the Rev James Scott, minister of Junction Road UF Church, and this was followed by a public meeting the following Thursday evening in the Great Wellington Street Hall. This occasion was remarkable not just for the warmth and enthusiasm shown for a minister who had over twenty-five years endeared himself to this vast congregation by his hard work, his pastoral concern, his common sense and firm leadership, it was even more remarkable as an exhibition of inter-denominational friendship and co-operation, in vivid contrast to the bitterness of the 1840s. It was just nine years since the Free Church and the United Presbyterians had joined together to form the United Free Church; and now, celebrating the parish minister's semi-jubilee, the thanksgiving service was led, not by another parish minister, but by the minister of a neighbouring UF church—an early example of that ecumenical spirit which was to characterize the second half of the twentieth century. Jimmie Scott himself was a well-known and influential minister in Leith, and a wit, whose church in Junction Road was for long after his death still known as 'Scott's Kirk'.

The meeting in the church hall was attended by a wide representation from the churches and public bodies in Leith. Provost Malcolm Smith, the Rev John White of South Leith, the Rev Thomas Crerar of North Leith UF (later St Nicholas) Church, the Rev Dr Hoernle of St James's Episcopal Church, the Rev J D Robertson of Ebenezer Church, the Rev David Robb of the Congregational Church all gave addresses of congratulation, and the speech of the evening was delivered by Lord Salvesen, who from his youth had been connected with North Leith Church.

A few months later Great Wellington Street became part of Summerside Place, and the kirk session then renamed the Hall North Leith Parish Church Hall. The following year, 1910 was notable for the installation of a stained glass window to commemorate Mr McCulloch's semi-jubilee, and just six weeks later King Edward died and the nation went into mourning. The pulpit and galleries were draped in purple and black, and these hangings were provided by Robert Maule & Son of Tolbooth Wynd (later at Edinburgh's West End, where the House of Fraser now operate) at a cost of £5.

At the age of fifty-nine John McCulloch was still energetically fulfilling his role as a leader in the community. In August 1911 the annual meeting of the North Leith heritors was held, and the parish minister attended as usual, representing the interests of the kirk session and congregation. After the annual report had been made comments were called for, and Mr McCulloch asked why certain repairs to the church, reported to the heritors fifteen months previously, had not yet been attended to. The chairman of the meeting, ex-Bailie Baxter, then launched into a long tirade against Mr McCulloch and the church, and gave no satisfactory explanation for the delay, which in fact appeared to have been due to his own dilatoriness. This storm in a teacup would hardly have been worth attention but for the light it throws on the character of Bailie Baxter. He was a stone-mason and builder, and a public-spirited man who gave much valuable service to Leith; but he was extremely irascible, and when roused would listen to nobody until he had had his say and simmered down. When Germany invaded Belgium in 1914 Bailie Baxter carved his own opinion of the event on a sandstone block, showing a scene of brutality under the inscription, 'The Valour of German Culture 1914'. This was mounted over a garage doorway in Pitt Street, and remains Bailie Baxter's memorial.

Mr McCulloch's health began to fail in 1912, and after a long illness he died in October that year. The vacancy was filled without delay, and in March 1913 the Rev James Roberston Sweet Wilson of St Columba's Church, Oban was inducted to the charge of North Leith, where he ministered for the rest of his life—twenty-nine years of unremitting, energetic service to the Church. And for James Wilson the Church meant not just North Leith congregation but the Church of Scotland. J R S Wilson built a reputation throughout Scotland as an able, effective evangelist, who was in demand as a speaker in widely scattered towns. When he took over in Leith in the spring of 1913 the membership of the congregation had diminished somewhat since the peak years at the beginning of the century, but the total still exceeded 2300, which represented a full load for the minister. Considerable reserves of energy were needed to fulfil the demands of nation-wide evangelism, added to the cares of a parish and congregation.

A sign of the times was the installation of a telephone at the manse shortly after Mr Wilson's arrival, when domestic phones were still comparatively rare. The new minister's interest in evangelism was soon apparent, for in January 1914 he welcomed a service in the church on a Tuesday evening as part of the Chapman-Alexander Campaign. On a Sunday afternoon the following May the church was the focus for a Children's Joint Missionary Service. The church and halls were accommodating more and more meetings, and it was becoming customary to have tea at many meetings. Domestic help was then much more readily available than now, and the ladies of the congregation took a poor view of the need to wash and dry the dishes. Rather than undertake this chore themselves they agreed to pay Mrs Potter the hall-keeper's wife 1/- (5p) for each time she washed and dried the dishes after a meeting. They surely got value for money!

The outbreak of war brought to every home a sense of continuing crisis. No one knew what tomorrow might bring. By the spring of 1915 it was generally realized that the war would probably last a long time. The cost of living had risen dramatically, and it was decided to increase the monthly pension paid to Poor Old Communicants from 3/- to 4/-. The Gretna Disaster in May 1915, in which the local regiment, the

7th Royal Scots, was decimated by the greatest disaster in railway history, appalled the town of Leith, and fourteen men connected with North Leith congregation were either missing, killed or injured. On Sunday evening 2 April 1916 the war arrived in Leith itself, when a Zeppelin dropped a bomb on the town. The minister of St Thomas parish church was conducting the evening service at North Leith when the bomb fell and destroyed his manse. Mr B M Murray, one of the deacons, also suffered the loss of his house that night, so not everyone in the congregation was able to rejoice and celebrate the centenary of the opening of the church. The celebration simply consisted of a thanksgiving service on 1 September 1916, conducted by one of the leading figures in the Church, the Very Rev A Wallace Williamson, minister of the High Kirk of St Giles, Chaplain-in-Ordinary to the King, and Dean of the Thistle and Chapel Royal, who still counted many friends in North Leith. One interesting feature in that service was the use of the kirk session of eleven of the twelve Bibles presented to the elders by Dr Johnston in 1816 on the occasion of the opening of the church.

The war brought many changes and adjustments in congregational life, and many ingrained habits and attitudes were ignored in response to the exigences of war. On Christmas Eve 1914 the hall was opened for the entertainment of the troops. North Leith Church had always had a close association with the garrison at Leith Fort. Regular church parades had always been held, and certain pews were traditionally reserved for the soldiers. Whether the opening of the hall on Christmas Eve had originally been meant only as a general gesture is not clear, but it was an immense success, and from that first night the hall opened every night until May 1915, when it closed for the summer months. Resuming again in the autumn the canteen at the hall remained a feature of North Leith until the end of February 1919. It was organized by the ladies of the congregation, who also opened a recreation room at Leith Fort, where a gymnasium was equipped and greatly enjoyed.

Those were the heydays of children's kinderspiels, and the children of the congregation did so well in the church hall that their efforts were repeated at the Alhambra Theatre in aid of the Prisoners-of-War fund. Nor was the minister to be outdone. He arranged for a garden party in the manse grounds in aid of the Red Cross Society, and this raised the impressive sum of £256. Perhaps impressed by the continued success of the soldiers' club in the church hall, Mr Lethem in October 1918 announced his intention of starting a boys' club in connection with the BBs. He secured premises in Coburg Street, where he hoped to open before the end of November, but before then the Armistice was announced.

A well-attended thanksgiving service was held at eight o'clock on the evening of 11 November 1918, and thereafter, with immense relief, the congregation turned to the business of refashioning their own corner of the new world their men had been fighting for. One of the first changes the kirk session considered was the appointment of women as deacons. During the war the women of the congregation displayed various talents they had never before had the opportunity of exercising. Bringing some of them into the Deacons' Court would at least be a first step towards recognizing their worth in managing the affairs of the congregation. Having decided in favour of this development, the session intimated their intention to the presbytery.

The war had encouraged new ideas. Playing host to the troops in the hall had broadened the outlook of many church members. Dancing and whist were now permitted on church premises, although one of the deacons sent in his resignation over that issue. Mr Wilson pointed out that despite the distaste of any older people for these innovations, they were, after all, innocent diversions enjoyed by the younger generation, and the session had agreed to make no objection. In December 1920 the congregational war memorial was dedicated, but there was a feeling that after the sorrows and sufferings of war a more cheerful attitude to life was called for. It was agreed to drop the practice of playing the 'Dead March' at memorial services for deceased elders. The parish sister, Miss Gold, organized an outing for old folks, and for the first time, in June 1920, the kirk session took note of a Sunday school trip to Dundas Castle. It was a very large and complicated exercise to transport the huge Sunday school. The hundreds of children were taken to Kirkliston in a convoy of motor lorries, and two four-in-hand coaches. For that generation of children the great thrill was to ride in a motor lorry: for their grandchildren the thrill would be to travel in a four-in-hand coach. At that period also, a more down-to-earth idea was tried out. During the summer months the offerings fell away sharply as people went on holiday, and the kirk session suggested that it would be a good idea for people on their return from holiday to put the offerings they would have contributed had they been at home into a special enveloped marked 'Holiday Offerings'. This did not work. People returning from holiday seldom had any money to spare. Post-war ideas of spare time activities also saw the demise of the Sunday Morning Fellowship Association, and the Literary Society. Membership dwindled and interest flagged until they were quietly abandoned, although the Literary Society was revived some years later.

Towards the end of 1922 the minister informed the session that he was approaching the heritors and asking them to sell the manse and find him a more suitable house. The session unanimously expressed their sympathy with Mr Wilson, and the session clerk informed the clerk to the heritors that the proposal had the full backing of the kirk session.

The manse was still Leith Mount, which had been acquired by the heritors in the 1860s. This Georgian villa stood in its own grounds on the corner of land where Ferry Road and North Junction Street met, and here, in recent years, Mr Wilson had held several garden parties to raise money. But in the course of over half a century the nature of the neighbourhood had changed. The North Junction Street tenements had been built, and just before the war the David Kilpatrick school had been erected, and occupied by troops while hostilities lasted. After the Armistice it came into use as a school, and as the area would almost certainly become even more congested in time to come it seemed advisable to find another manse in a residential part of the parish.

There followed an unfortunate sequence of events. From the first the kirk session misunderstood their standing in the matter, but both the minister and the presbytery officials were disingenuous in their dealings with the elders. There was no difficulty in finding a purchaser for Leith Mount. The town council offered £3500 for the house and grounds, and this was accepted. Finding another suitable manse was more complicated, as the choice would have to satisfy the minister, the heritors, the kirk session and the presbytery.

A house in Lomond Road came on the market. Mr Wilson inspected it and decided it would make an ideal manse. When the kirk session heard of this they unanimously disapproved, and intimated their opposition to the clerk to the heritors. Lomond Road was within the parish, but was only yards from the western boundary—a ridiculous situation for the North Leith manse. Mr Wilson claimed it was only nine minutes' walk from the car termimus at Stanley Road, but it would require a very athletic walker to cover the distance in that time. The heritors met the kirk session and explained their difficulty in finding a house which would satisfy all four interested parties. The kirk session then asked the minister what his requirements would be in a house suitable for a manse. He did not answer directly, but said he had consulted the presbytery for guidance on what would be essential features in a manse for North Leith. In answer the presbytery said the manse must be within the parish, there must be immediate right of entry; it must contain six bedrooms, three public rooms, bathroom, kitchen offices and servants' accommodation; and it must have a garden. Also the price must allow of the heritors redeeming the feu duty.

This information being passed to the kirk session, they advertised for a suitable house, and from the replies selected six houses within the parish and much nearer the church than

Lomond Road. This list was passed to Mr Wilson with a request that he might make a choice of one of these houses. Mr Wilson handed the list to the presbytery without considering any of the proposed houses, and then wrote to the heritors asking them to secure an option to purchase the Lomond Road house, and that they need expect no further opposition from the session, who would concur with the presbytery's decision. Learning of these manoeuvres the kirk session again wrote the clerk to the heritors repeating their unanimous and unalterable opposition to the house in Lomond Road, as being much too far away from the church. The minister then informed the session that in fact they had no standing in the purchase of a manse a matter which concerned the heritors and presbytery alone. This shocked the kirk session: it was a complete reversal of what both heritors and session had hitherto understood, namely, that four parties were involved and ought all to be satisfied in the matter of the new manse. The session appealed to the presbytery, but to no avail. The Lomond Road house became the manse; from first to last it proved inconvenient, and after the Union of Churches in 1929 it was located well outside the parish.

When the union of the Established Church and the United Free Church took place there were great official celebrations, and many columns of newsprint devoted to the occasion, but congregational life was not greatly affected. Union had been discussed for years, and North Leith, like other congregations, had long since approved. They had long been on very good terms with the local UF churches, and as far as ordinary members were concerned union might quite easily have been achieved immediately after the war. But the leaders were concerned with legal and theological issues—with the fine print, as it were, and the Union was the fruit of very long and intricate negotiations. Congregations were affected mainly in two ways. It became necessary for many to change their names. North Leith UF Church could not simply drop the 'UF' and call itself North Leith Church, so it became St Nicholas, after the old St Nicholas Chapel. The presbytery at first decided that North Leith Parish Church would drop the word 'Parish'; but later, advised by an Assembly committeed, 'Parish' was restored, to the general satisfaction. The other big change was the need to redraw parish boundaries, as, from the time of the Union, every congregation would require to have a parish responsibility. This presented no great problem in rural areas, but led to many ridiculous rearrangements of parish bounds in the cities. But there was real determination that the Union, so obviously desirable, should not be allowed to break down on the practical level, and there was general acceptance of the new parish bounds as a kind of makeshift which would become meaningful as further adjustments were made when many inevitable unions of congregations took place.

CHAPTER 8

The People's Kirk in a Changing Society

The union of the Churches in 1929 took place in the midst of severe economic depression—a time of great poverty and hardship. A considerable number of Church members were living on the dole, and while the whole country suffered, Leith had the melancholy distinction of being an unemployment 'blackspot'. At the beginning of 1934 North Leith Church took over a house in Industry Lane and opened a soup kitchen there. The church officer, assisted by a rota of ladies from the congregation, was in daily attendance there, serving between twenty-five and thirty 'regulars'. This reversion to a practice of Victorian and Edwardian times brought many sour reflections on the Great War and the promises of better times to follow. There was no money to spare. Those who had a job and a steady income, even a small income, were reckoned fortunate. The Revised Church Hymnary had been published in 1927, but it was taken up slowly. The elders talked about the new book, but:

> owing to the present depression the Psalmody Committee recommend we continue the present hymnary meantime, but suggest both numbers be read out, from the present hymnary and the new one.

Those who could afford it and were interested, bought the Revised Hymnary, but none of the new hymns were used. This went on until 1933, when it became impossible to buy new copies of the old hymn book. For another two years the old books were still in use, becoming ever more dog-eared and grubby. On Sunday 6 October 1935 the Revised Hymnary was at last adopted for use in North Leith Church.

The kirk session evinced a willingness to accept change, and even to institute new developments, but this went along with a determination to hold fast to long-standing traditions and patterns of thinking. In 1931 the Literary Society reported that it was defunct, at least in its original form; but there was a growing interest in amateur drama. Would the kirk session agree to the society starting up a dramatic section? No, the kirk session would not agree to any such thing. They were prepared to sanction a Literary Society, but no drama. This was the attitude of the Kirk in the eighteenth century when John Home's tragedy 'Douglas' was produced in the Edinburgh Theatre—and John Home was a Leith man.

In that same year a proposal to introduce unfermented wine at Communion was defeated by fifteen votes to nine—an emphatic majority. But this time the kirk session was facing a much more powerful body of opinion in the congregation than the young people in the Literary Society. The Woman's Guild at once took the matter up and organized a petition which they presented to the kirk session early in 1932. The session clerk reported that ninety members of the Guild had signed the petition asking for unfermented wine. The elders hummed and hawed and postponed a decision 'to a later date'. With their wives pressing for an answer, the issue was thoroughly discussed two months later and it was agreed as an experiment to hold a communion service on the last Sunday of January 1933, when unfermented wine would be used. In order to discover the strength of demand in the congregation, those wishing to attend would be issued with blank communion cards, on which they would write their name and address, and hand them in as they entered the church that day. In the event 339 members attended the two tables of that January communion. 'This was considered satisfactory, notwithstanding the inclement weather'. And for many years thereafter unfermented wine in January remained the practice. Taking his opportunity at this time, Mr Wilson, the minister, who was almost certainly in favour of unfermented wine, drew attention to the custom of the elders having spirits available at the lunch they shared between the two services on Communion Sunday. After discussion it was agreed to drop this in future, but to keep a bottle in the vestry 'for special use'.

Then there was the matter of the Ladies Badminton Club, which showed both sides of the kirk session's attitude to life in the church. Approval was given to the formation of this club in 1932. It was a new development—modern and exciting. But there had to be strict rules—necessary rules about the use of the halls, payment for heating and lighting, payment for their own equipment, consideration for other organizations using the premises. The elders also insisted that only ladies of twenty years old and upwards could be members. Only those who were regular workers or leaders in other congregational activities could be allowed to play badminton. And anyone giving up their work in other church organizations must automatically cease to be a member of the Badminton Club. Also the club must have no more than twenty-four members. These restrictions might well have dampened youthful enthusiasm.

Seen from a distance of sixty years all this may seem amusing, but middle-aged people in the 'thirties had been Victorian children who in their lifetime had seen immense changes in the society they had once known, and were wrestling with the problems and dilemmas of holding to their Christian faith, and presenting it as attractive to a generation devastated by war and unemployment. The parish was now much smaller than it had been. After the 1929 Union of the Churches the new bounds were:

Starting from Anchorfield Bridge, the boundary proceeds southwards along the centre lines of George Street and North Fort Street to the centre line of Ferry Road, thence

eastwards along the centre line of Ferry Road to the centre
line of Junction Street, but excluding St. Nicholas Church
and ground surrounding. The boundary thence proceeds
northwards along the centre line of North Junction Street.

This smaller parish area certainly made adequate pastoral care
more possible than formerly, and Mr Wilson was soon
organizing the visitation of every house in the parish. Mr
E J P Gregory, one of the elders, arranged for open-air
meetings each Sunday evening in August 1932 at the corner
of Fort Place and Hamilton Street. In the winter of 1933–4
the Leith churches booked the Alhambra Theatre on Sunday
evenings for three months:

> to hold religious services for the very poor, the un-
> employed, and those people whom the Church does not
> reach through our ordinary church services.

These theatre meetings were well attended, but expensive to
organize. It was an era of evangelistic meetings, in which Mr
Wilson was very active.

In those days the Armistice was remembered with two
minutes' silence on 11 November, but there were mixed
feelings about having a Sunday service relating to that event.
In November 1936, just eight years after the ending of
the Great War, Mr Wilson paid no attention to the
commemoration and conducted the normal church services.
At the December session meeting he was taken to task.
He explained that the Church recognized no official
Remembrance Day, and the matter of a church service was
left to the discretion of parish ministers. After the experience
of the years immediately following the Armistice, he himself
thought the holding of a remembrance service was keeping
many people away from church as it brought back such
harrowing memories. The session were divided on the matter
and it was left for a decision the following year.

In the summer of 1938 Mr Wilson realized a long-standing

ambition, when a country cottage was acquired to be used as a holiday home for old folk in the congregation. Anwoth Cottage, at Newbigging, near Carnwath, was bought for £120, and of that sum £100 was donated by Mr Pourie, one of the elders. After some initial doubts about its distance from Leith, the cottage soon proved a boon. Seventy old people enjoyed a holiday there that first summer of 1938, and despite the shorter season with the onset of war, over fifty more benefited in 1939. Through the war and early post-war years Anwoth Cottage continued as a blessing to many of the poorer members, but with rising costs the house was sold in 1951 for £250 and the money added to the fund held for the benefit of the poor.

The outbreak of war had a much more immediate effect on church life than in 1914. Families were disrupted with the evacuation of children, all premises in use had to be blacked-out, and congregational activities had to adapt to the halls being used as an ARP post. Evening services were held in the blacked-out halls, and after negotiating with various authorities the ARP found other accommodation. The Infantry Records Office also cast eyes on the Summerside Place halls for use as offices, but that threat also passed off. Morning services continued to be held in church, but with the possibility of an air-raid warning interrupting the service, arrangements had to be made for evacuating the congregation to suitable shelter. It was agreed that people in the gallery would leave by the front door, and those in the area by the back doors, all to make their way to the vaults under the church, although the minister thought it might be safe enough to stand under the galleries. We were still naive in these matters in 1939.

After the early excitement, the 'phoney war' of 1939–40 was followed by the evacuation of Dunkirk, and in the autumn of 1940 by the Battle of Britain. The action, the fighting, the attacks on civilian targets all seemed to be concentrated on the south—far enough from Leith; but in April 1941 the war suddenly arrived in our midst when a landmine shattered a large area in North Leith. Families in Prince Regent Street lost their homes, the town hall was shattered, and the church suffered damage from blast. Worship continued in the hall. All the life of the congregation was affected to a greater or lesser extent. Office bearers, leaders and active members learned what it meant to 'make do and mend', and the upsets, difficulties and frustrations were accepted with a shrug, and the cliche of those days 'There's a war on'.

Having adapted to the situation following war damage, the congregation in March 1942 suffered the double blow of the minister's death and the session clerk's resignation. Mr Wilson had ministered in North Leith for twenty-nine years. He had provided strong leadership since 1913, he was a fervent evangelical preacher, known throughout Scotland for his part in campaigns all over the country, and he was respected for his pastoral diligence. His death created a vacancy which caused much anxiety, for it would surely take an exceptional man to accept the challenge of a ministry in a large city parish with a damaged church and other stricken buildings, and the many pastoral problems thrown up by the war. William Robertson the session clerk was no longer living in Leith, and the war-time difficulties of running his business left him too little time for the duties of his office. Fortunately Mr Hugh McPhie accepted the post and was at once immersed in much correspondence and many meetings.

The Rev Samuel Knox, the assistant minister, agreed to remain as *locum tenens* during the vacancy. The kirk session then had two pressing matters requiring attention before the vacancy could be filled. At the Union of the Churches in 1929 it was agreed that the large endowments enjoyed by many of the old parish churches should be reduced and the money thus released used to benefit many of the former UF churches who struggled to support a minister with little or no endowment. Nothing would be rushed, but when the first vacancy occurred in an Established Church congregation the opportunity would be taken to make an appropriate reduction in the endowments held in that parish. Mr Wilson's death caused the first vacancy in North Leith since 1929, so a committee from the presbytery met with the kirk session. It had become generally accepted that a parish church of the old establishment should part with two-sevenths of the endowments, and this reduction would be made up from congregational offerings. This worried the elders. In normal circumstances there would have been no objection, but in war-time, with services in the hall instead of the church, attendance was badly affected, and congregational offerings had slumped. They argued that the matter should be left till after the war, but the presbytery saw things differently, as other churches all over the country were also suffering. A compromise was reached. A reduction in endowment was agreed, but not the whole two-sevenths.

The other pressing matter was the manse. Mr Wilson's house was no longer in the parish, and it was in such a bad state of repair that the Ministry of Works and Buildings would probably not permit the needful money to be spent on it. Fortunately Cairnie Lodge at 11 Summerside Place happened to be vacant just then. This had been the home of Captain Ewing, one of the elders, and it was in excellent repair. While not strictly within the new parish bounds, it was but ten minutes' walk from the church, and with consent of the presbytery it was purchased.

The Rev Hugh Osborne Douglas MA of St John's Church, Leven, was named as sole nominee, and he was inducted to the vacant charge in November 1942. One of the first matters the new minister addressed himself to was the level of weekly offerings in the congregation. Like most parish churches with large endowments, there had never been much pressure on the people to make adequate offerings in church. The minister pointed out that North Leith was mainly supported by 310 members, and that this would have to change rapidly. Having viewed the extent of the war damage he realized that Government help would come far short of what would be needed to restore that fine building in Madeira Street. And with many important decisions to be made he found another anomaly in North Leith. This was the Deacons' Court. Deacons' Courts were the hallmark of the UF Church: they had operated in the Free Church since the Disruption. Some years later this peculiarity of North Leith was remarked on by a Quinquennial Committee visiting:

> The Committee were especially interested in the existence of a Deacons' Courth in this *quoad omnia* parish, this court helping in administering benevolence and sitting in with the session at its meetings, affording an excellent training for the eldership . . .

That was true: elders in North Leith were generally elected from among members of the Deacons' Court. Mr Douglas as a newcomer however, was not clear as to the standing of deacons attending session meetings, and with many important matters likely to be requiring the session's attention and decision before long, he had a meeting with the deacons, pointing out that while they were welcome to session meetings, they could have no vote there.

As a member of the Iona Community Mr Douglas was closely associated with the Rev George MacLeod (later Lord MacLeod) the founder of the community, and they shared views on management and method in the Church. Mr Douglas very soon got the elders to discard much of the formalism associated with session meetings, and to address each other by their Christian names. But other ministers had other ideas. When Mr Todd arrived in 1960 he soon put a stop to that and got the elders to revert to the old formalism of addressing each other as 'Mr'. The members of session presumably shrugged their shoulders and complied, no doubt thinking their own thoughts about 'thae meenisters'.

Morning worship resumed in the church, and an assistant was sought. Mr Knox, who had remained as locum during the vacancy, had gone to Stichill, near Kelso, just before Mr Douglas arrived. Assistants were hard to come by, but Mr Whiteford, minister at St Andrews Place Church, who had been interim moderator, had a son in the RAF who, having completed his training for the ministry, had joined the RAF as a combatant officer. He now offered his services as a chaplain, and after his discharge from combatant duties he would be available to serve as assistant at North Leith before taking up his appointment as a chaplain. This was good news at a difficult time for the congregation, and in fact it was only at the end of November 1943 that David Whiteford was ordained in North Leith Church to serve as a chaplain in the RAF.

The parish bounds were again altered in June 1943, when there was added to the parish the odd numbers in North Fort Street, Hawthornbank Terrace and Place, the south side of Dudley Bank, Industry Lane, Lapicide Place and Wilkie Place.

Despite the difficulty of finding leaders under wartime conditions the Girl Guide company was carrying the permitted maximum of fifty girls, and a branch of the Girls' Guildry was started. The Boys' Brigade company celebrated its jubilee in 1944, when many of the elders, themselves Old Boys, shared a celebration supper with the present officers and senior boys. Other changes and developments marked those war-time years, when so many activities had to be curtailed, so many plans postponed. At the beginning of 1944 it was agreed to discontinue the January communion with unfermented wine: thenceforward there would be three communions in the year—at Easter, the last Sunday in October, and on the Sunday nearest Christmas—with seats set apart for those wishing unfermented wine. A watchnight service was held on Christmas Eve for the first time in 1943, and in 1944 evening services throughout Holy Week were introduced. The session had not agreed to a Whitsunday communion when the minister had first suggested it in 1944, but two years later this service was established without any dissentient. VE Day was marked by an evening service of thanksgiving, and while hostilities still continued in the Far East it was felt that VE Day virtually marked the end of the war, and everyone was eager to return to a more normal life.

A broadcast service from the church in October 1945 was felt to mark the end of wartime tensions and traumas and was an occasion of warm thanksgiving.

A month later the presbytery asked for discussion in the congregations on the question of appointing women elders. At a congregational meeting thirteen members voted in favour of the proposal and seventy-seven against; and the kirk session likewise turned it down by fifteen votes to three. This was in line with feeling in the Church generally at that time.

The chief concern of the congregation just then, however, was the need to have the church restored and made fit for public worship again. A committee formed in 1944 had been at work before the end of the war, assessing what would have to be done, and considering how to build up a fund to meet what was realized would be a very large expenditure. The War Damage Commission would make a contribution towards essential repairs, but the kirk session felt that now, if ever, a general restoration and refurbishment of the whole building should be considered. The minister approached Major Ian Lindsay, the architect in charge of the restoration of Iona Abbey, asking him to come to North Leith, view the building, and offer his ideas on what might be made of the war-damaged church. By the summer of 1946 Mr Lindsay produced suggested plans for the church, which included the removal of the organ to the gallery, a new pulpit, alteration to the seating, and repainting the whole of the interior. Cost was estimated at £6150.

In November 1946 the congregation agreed that the architect's proposals be accepted, although doubts were expressed over some items. The air-raid shelters erected round the church were by then being removed by the town and the ground restored to something like its former appearance. Restoration of the building began, and with the roof in a dangerous state, and the whole structure affected by blast, progress at first was slow. Work began on 1 June 1948, and by then rising costs necessitated a revised estimate of £8619. The Baird Trust promised a grant of £1600, on condition that no debt was incurred in having the work done, and that everything should be finished by 15 May 1949. This deadline proved impossible to meet, although the work went on steadily. The Baird Trustees agreed to extend the time for completion of the work by a year. By the autumn of 1949 the estimated cost, with some necessary repairs to the manse, had risen to £10,593. On appeal the Baird Trustees increased their grant, and the great project was finished and the church reopened for public worship on 13 May 1950, the Rev Dr George MacLeod preaching on that occasion.

The restored building really looked like a new church. The pastel-coloured woodwork and the clear glass in the windows brought a dazzling light and sense of airiness to the interior. The effect was sensational in Church circles and North Leith was the centre of interest and attention in the presbytery. Somewhat surprisingly, in view of the departure from tradition in the decoration of the church, the kirk session decided to continue charging seat rent in the newly refurbished church. A flat rate of 10/- a year was set, and 582 seats were quickly taken up. It was to be another eleven years before it was decided to abolish this antiquated system of generating income for the church.

In June of the following year Mr Douglas accepted a call to St Mary's, Dundee. There was general regret at his departure so soon after the restoration of the church, but the minister felt he had completed a significant piece of work in Leith, and was ready for the opportunity of a new and very different charge. After a vacancy of nine months the Rev John H Gibson was inducted to the charge in May 1952. There may have been a feeling of anti-climax in the congregation when Mr Gibson took over. After the long struggle to pay for the restoration, and then Mr Douglas's departure, there was no obvious challenge left to face. One thing however did rouse Mr Gibson and the elders. There was one derelict area in the midst of the parish where nothing was being done. The same blast which had so damaged the church had also wrought havoc in the surrounding area. Leith Town Hall had been badly damaged, and stood as a useless ruin, and nothing was being done about it. In November 1952 the session clerk was directed to write to Mr James Hoy, MP for Leith, drawing attention to the need for the Town Hall to be restored. It took another ten years for this to be done, but the kirk session of North Leith made one of the first protests and calls for action in that neglected central site in the parish.

1956 marked the 350 anniversary of the Act of Parliament establishing the parish of North Leith, and on 13 May this was celebrated. As that date was also the sixth anniversary of the reopening of the church after the restoration, it was an outstanding celebration. Mr Hugh Douglas came from Dundee to preach at the morning service, and in the afternoon a procession of the young people of the church came from the old St Ninian's Church, by way of Coburg Street, North Junction Street and Prince Regent Street to Madeira Street, where Mr Gibson conducted a service.

But the times were changing. The advent of black-and-white television was at least one factor leading to the demise of the evening service in many churches. Attendance at North Leith dwindled to the extent that in January 1957 the minister appealed to the kirk session to support the evening service with their families, but to little effect. But while they did not attend these services the elders would not abandon them. A change of minister made no difference. Mr Gibson's successors could not halt the ebbing tide. These services were transferred to the chapel, reduced to one per month, and abandoned in summer; but nothing could alter the fact that in Leith one diet of worship on a Sunday was as much as the people would support.

This was but one symptom of the vast changes taking place in the town, and it was in Mr Gibson's time that these changes were becoming evident, and escalating. With the collapse of heavy industries, employing many hundreds of men, massive unemployment returned to the port as in the inter-war period. The search for work took young people especially away from the town. At the same time the need for slum clearance and the provision of new housing led to the development of numerous housing schemes all round Edinburgh and many Leith families moved unwillingly from the port. The life of the congregation was severely affected by these developments, as fewer and fewer young people were to be found in the parish, and more and more of the members became resident quite far from the church in various housing schemes. This in turn led to fewer members attending as regularly as they had done when living in the parish; and good, faithful members still living in the parish and adjacent areas, were steadily becoming more elderly. In Mr McCulloch's time anything from forty to sixty First Communicants were admitted at the spring and autumn sacraments, but the Leith which had produced these figures had gone for ever, and a large number of the tenements which had housed the people then had been demolished. Mr Gibson was the first of the North Leith ministers to feel the cold draught of Leith's transformation.

One notable thing at least was achieved during his ministry. After many years of complaint by successive organists, the organ was at last cleaned, restored and electrified. It was an expensive operation costing £1668, but the result was highly satisfactory. The next year Mr Gibson demitted his office as parish minister on his appointment as full-time chaplain at Crichton Royal Mental Hospital at Dumfries.

During the vacancy that followed the kirk session was approached by a deputation from the presbytery asking for their views on a possible union with St Ninian's Coburg Street Church. The declining population in Leith, with the extensive demolition of housing, had affected every congregation in the town, and the presbytery was anxious to redeploy the Church's resources to meet the changing situation. But the kirk session pointed out that a simple union of congregations would not provide any answer to the problems facing parish and congregation. There were still 1300 members in North Leith Church, and in the way things had developed in the town a rapidly increasing proportion of the congregation was elderly and frail. These people required far more pastoral care than the young and middle-aged, and the number of funerals was much higher than in a younger congregation. The result was a heavy workload for the minister. To increase the size of the congregation by adding more elderly folk from the same community would be unrealistic without more ministerial assistance—and the shortage of ministers was the main reason for the current approach from the presbytery. As there seemed to be no adequate answer to these difficulties in the meantime, the matter was dropped.

Andrew Stewart Todd was inducted as minister of North Leith in June 1960, and at his first session meeting a letter was read from Mr W S Gavin resigning from the captaincy of the 1st Leith BB Company on account of ill-health. He had served the company for almost half a century, proving a worthy successor to Mr Lethem. His kind of absorbed devotion to the BB however, made it difficult to find a young man with that kind of enthusiasm, and enough spare time to spend in that service. Ian Anderson took charge as a kind of interim captain for a year, before Gregor Cowan stepped into the breach.

The rapid and continuing movement of population away from the port made the roll-keeper's task difficult. Shortly after Mr Todd's arrival it was reported that over fifty members had disappeared. They had moved, or had been moved from Leith and had omitted to leave their new address. Another aspect of the same problem was poorer attendances at church, as younger people with their children moved to the housing schemes, from which public transport was often inadequate on a Sunday, while the elderly tended more and more to be fair weather attenders, which was understandable. Also related to this situation was a decision by the kirk session to make use of a bequest of £1000—the Reid Bequest—to have the session hall converted to a chapel, to be used for smaller services, weddings and the like—subject to the cost being reasonable. Mr Todd was deeply interested in and know-ledgeable on church music, liturgy and artistic matters, and was later to have considerable influence in the preparation of the third edition of the Church Hymnary. He introduced a number of changes in the way the communion service was conducted, and at his instigation the proposal for a new chapel was referred to the Church's Advisory Committee on Artistic Questions. That body approved of the proposal and suggested the session should call on Mr Ian Lindsay again, who had planned the restoration of the church. This was done, and in the autumn of 1961 Mr Lindsay produced plans which, after detailed examination, were accepted, and the Reid Memorial Chapel was opened on Sunday 10 February 1963.

In the summer of 1961 the kirk session was planning a Christian Stewardship Campaign to meet the challenge of the changing nature of the community when a new development brought a fresh complication to the situation. The Rev Walter Taverner, minister of the adjacent parish of St Nicholas, retired at the end of June, creating a new vacancy in the North Leith area. In the following December the Rev Alexander Walker of St Ninian's Coburg Street departed for a Glasgow church, and the union of these two congregations was seen to be inevitable. Neither had the numerical strength of North Leith, and in June 1962 the Rev David Logan was inducted to the united charge of St Ninian's Ferry Road.

The parish church still had a large congregation, although facing great social problems. In February 1962 a quinquennial visitation committee from the prebystery reported on North Leith, taking notice of the Christian Stewardship Campaign:

There are 400 elderly people in this congregation of 1200. Further, a large percentage of the congregation live at a considerable distance from the church and outwith the parish bounds. An assistant minister is engaged in the work ... but the kirk session expresses the opinion that the services of a deaconess would be of great value ... Since the beginning of the Christian Stewardship Campaign in October 1961, 700 commitment cards have been received, from which it appears that forty are willing to undertake hospital and sick visitation, eighty are prepared to visit elderly and lonely, thirty-five offer transport to church for the infirm, and sixteen will baby-sit to facilitate attendance at divine worship. Daily intercessory prayer will be offered by 200, while twenty-five wish to join a Bible study group. The Committee feel that these figures indicate a promising future for North Leith.

Whatever the future might hold, there appeared to be a lively, committed heart to the congregation.

Mr Todd's interest in Church music was soon evident in congregational worship. It was his idea to have a production of Benjamin Britten's version of the Chester miracle play *Noye's Fludde*, and this took place in the church on 18 January 1965, with the assistance of the organist, William Stevenson, Sunday School children and some members of the congregation. Nine hundred and thirty people were present to see the performance that evening, when the final highlight was the appearance of a large rainbow, stretched in a perfect arc between the north and south galleries. This event was an effective stimulant for the congregation amid many depressing changes in the parish.

A parish census in 1966 produced some interesting statistics:

	Adults	*Children*
Members of North Leith Parish Church	295	136
Members of other Churches of Scotland	985	331
Members of other Protestant churches . .	330	77
Members of R C Church	346	98
Non-members	720	296
	2646	938

More than a quarter of the parish population claimed no church connection, but of the remaining three-quarters the proportion of active members in any congregation remained quite obscure. In North Leith parish church however, speculation had to be laid aside the next year when Mr Todd announced his call to be minister of St Machar's in Aberdeen. His seven years in Leith had been spent with a committed fellowship of Christians striving to cope with their situation in a town where changes continued with bewildering speed. The population had been reduced to two-thirds of what it had been at the close of the war in 1945, and was still reducing steadily. Not only houses but also businesses had been forced to close or transfer elsewhere, and in the last three years of Mr Todd's ministry work had been proceeding with the destruction of the very heart of Old Leith, and the future for the town was unpredictable.

This time the presbytery proposed a union with Bonnington Church, and the adoption of the 'Model Constitution'. This in fact would mean the abolition of the Deacons' Court, and in its place the creation of a Congregational Board. As the proposed union was to be between a *quoad omnia* parish church and a former UP congregation, the adoption of the Model Constitution was inevitable. North Leith congregation agreed to the union in November 1967, and the Rev Douglas Clarke, minister of Bonnington Church, was introduced as minister of the united charge at the end of January 1968.

Bonnington UP Church was first opened for public worship in April 1880, and from the start there was a close association with the parish church. On more than one occasion around the turn of the century Bonnington congregation had had the use of the Great Wellington Street halls for concerts to raise money for various projects, and in the autumn of 1901 the Bonnington folk were given the use of the halls for over six weeks for Sunday worship while their own church was undergoing repair. Mr McCulloch had been on very friendly terms with the first two Bonnington ministers. These had both been outstanding men. Dr Hutchison, coming from Renfrew in 1877, had seen Bonnington Church erected, and ministered there while it rapidly grew in numbers as the population in the area increased steadily with extensive housing development. His successor, the Rev Robert Small, a scholarly man with rather uncertain health, became nationally known when he produced his *History of the Congregations of the United Presbyterian Church*—recognized since its publication as a standard work. By the time it appeared however, Mr Small had left Leith for a less demanding charge at North Berwick.

Typical of UP congregations, the Bonnington folk were strong advocates of the virtue of self-help, and ready at any cost to preserve that independence. But the changing circumstances of Leith had affected their prospects too, and union with a neighbouring Church of Scotland appeared eminently sensible. An indication of the forward-looking character of the Bonnington kirk session had been given in 1927, when the Assemblies of both Established and United Free Churches circularized congregations with the proposed Basis of Union of the two churches, asking for comments and suggestions for improving that Basis. Bonnington replied to the effect that while they were in agreement with the proposals generally, they thought the occasion of the Union would be a good time to introduce women to the eldership. This, of course, was ignored, as an unnecessary 'hot potato' at a time when the broadest basis of agreement was being sought, but it did mark the Bonnington elders as being somewhat ahead of their time in thinking about the Church's government and discipline.

North Leith and Bonnington Church had a membership totalling 1500, and the disposal of the Bonnington properties was a matter of immediate concern. North Leith manse was sold as Mr Clarke chose to remain in his own manse at 6 Craighall Gardens. Some of the pews of Bonnington Church were sold to Blackhall UF Church, and some pews and chairs were given to the Church for the Deaf and Dumb in Falkirk. The stained glass windows of the 1939–45 War Memorial were transferred to the North Leith chapel, and others disposed of to various churches. The building itself and the site on which it stood proved difficult to sell, and it was not until the spring of 1971 that the Anchor Company bought the church, demolished it, and erected a block of flats on the site.

The union did nothing to solve the social problems of the

area. Office-bearers and leaders of the various organizations were soon aware of this fact. A joint meeting of the kirk sessions of North Leith and Bonnington, and St Ninian's Ferry Road, discussed prospects for the Church in the district, but nothing positive came of that meeting. One thing was becoming clear, and that was the need for a young and active minister, and for young and active elders. Mr Clarke said he would be prepared to move if a young minister could be found, but at that period there were not many students coming into the Church from the four divinity colleges in Scotland. As for elders, in March 1973, Mr B J Bennett, pointing out the urgent need for new blood in the kirk session, moved for the appointment of women elders, but a decision was postponed for a year. Nothing was done for another three years, and in March 1976 the acute need for elders was again faced. This time not a single man approached had consented to his name being considered for the eldership, and the minister was then allowed to appeal once more from the pulpit for nominations to the kirk session, 'no reference to be made in the announcement as to sex'. This naturally produced no women elders, but one man was ordained later that year.

The onset of inflation now added another problem to the situation of the beleagured kirk session. The roll had now dropped to 769 members, and the presbytery's Unions and Readjustments Committee reported on the situation of North Leith and Bonnington:

Depopulation and the ageing of the remaining population has led to a reduction of membership, and this, with inflation, makes upkeep of fabric a pressing problem . . .

Almost two-thirds of the membership resides beyond the parish and continguous parishes . . . Since many are now elderly their attendance at Church can be irregular through infirmity or bad weather . . .

We are of opinion that this congregation is fulfilling its

purpose and that it needs encouragement and help in facing the challenge of developing new methods of witness and mission . . .

Mr J M Couper, a retired minister and former missionary, was appointed as part-time assistant, and the decision was taken to sell the halls at Summerside Place. In December 1978 representatives from the kirk session met with a similar group from St Ninian's Ferry Road, and from the presbytery's Unions and Readjustments, Maintenance of the Ministry, and Superintendence Committees, and it was then agreed to seek a union between the two congregations at some future date. On 10 June 1979 Edinburgh Presbytery approved a Basis of Deferred Union between North Leith and Bonnington and St Ninian's Ferry Road churches. Mr Clarke would resign his charge in the interest of readjustment in the area, and both congregations would unite in calling a minister who would be inducted to North Leith and Bonnington until such time as Mr Logan of St Ninian's Ferry Road retired. Thereafter the union would take effect and the new minister would become minister of the united charge. These arrangements went forward smoothly and in October 1980 the Rev William C Neill was inducted to North Leith and Bonnington Church.

The new minister, young and energetic, brought to the congregation an air of hope and expectancy. In six months after his arrival the saga of women elders was brought to an end, when ten new elders were ordained—nine of them women! Then Mr Logan retired on 13 June 1982, and Mr Neill became minister of the united charge of North Leith.

The congregation of St Ninian's Ferry Road had a mixed ancestry in several divisions within the Scottish Church, beginning in the early years of the nineteenth century. The Burgher Church of North Leith was formed from a group of members of the Burgher Church in the Kirkgate. Those living in North Leith wished to form a congregation of their own, and were allowed by their synod in 1816 to break away from the Kirkgate Church, probably because North Leith was showing signs of becoming a growth area. That was the year in which North Leith parish congregation moved from their original home by the river, and the Burgher people rented the old St Ninian's church from the parish kirk now in Madeira Street. They lost no time in having their own place of worship built, and in February 1819 they moved into their own ambitious building in Coburg Street, seated for 1100! Their minister was a remarkable young man called James Harper, who remained with the congregation for the next sixty years! In 1820 the Burghers and the Antiburghers joined together to form the United Associate Church, and in 1843 James Harper became Professor of Pastoral Theology at that church's divinity hall. Three years later he was made Professor of Systematic Theology, and in 1847, when the United Associate and Relief churches came together as the United Presbyterian Church, Professor Harper became Principal of the United Presbyterian Theological College, in the building well-known in Edinburgh as the Synod Hall in Castle Terrace. This academic career was pursued by Principal Harper while he still remained minister of his church in Coburg Street.

Another branch in the family tree of St Ninian's Ferry Road made its first appearance in 1821, when the Seamen's Friend Society were given an old naval hulk, which was moored in the Queen's Dock, known later as the West Old Dock. Here on Sundays were held services for seamen, and on weekdays a school, or Seamen's Academy was started. Adults and children alike were illiterate, but they eagerly grasped the opportunity of elementary education. A young divinity student, John Thomson, took this enterprise in hand, and remained with the seamen on the hulk after his licensing. In time the vessel became rotten and unsafe, but the Navy would not replace it. Thomson's work was greatly appreciated by the Seamen's Friend Society, however, and they had a church built at the corner of Dock Street and Commercial Street. The foundation stone was laid in May 1839, and the church opened for worship in 1840.

John Thomson still rated as a probationer or missionary,

but when the 'Mariners' Church' as it was popularly known, was opened, it was given the status of a *quoad sacra* church within the parish of North Leith, and John Thomson was ordained and inducted as the minister. At the Disruption the minister and the entire congregation joined the Free Church. For some unknown reason the Mariners' Free Kirk changed its name in 1867, and became known as St Ninian's Free, becoming St Ninian's UF in 1900. But for all that it remained for the people of Leith the 'Mariners' Kirk', no matter what later names it may have been given officially.

'Floating Johnnie' as he was known, remained with the Mariners' Kirk all his life. For over thirty years he was clerk of the Free Synod of Lothian and Tweeddale, and died in 1881. The Mariners' Kirk however was from its beginning more than a church, for the building also accommodated a school, and in that same building, after the passing of the First Merchant Shipping Act in 1854, a Nautical School was started for sailors. Previous to this there had been no official provision for the training of seamen. Boys went to sea and learned their craft from the rest of the crew. If they were lucky the master or mate would take an interest in them; otherwise they had no training, and theirs was a dangerous calling. The Merchant Shipping Act provided for courses for masters and mates leading to examinations for Board of Trade Certificates. 'Floating Johnnie' was appointed secretary to the Leith Nautical School at a fee of five guineas per annum. For the first few years the Nautical School had very mixed fortune, until in 1861 James Bolam came from Newcastle and devoted his life to what in time became Leith Nautical College.

With the union of the United Presbyterian Church and the Free Church in 1900, Coburg Street UP Church became Coburg UF Church, and Free St Ninian's became St Ninian's UF Church; and in 1929, with the union of the Established Church and the United Free Church, Coburg Street UF became Harper Memorial Church, and St Ninian's UF became Leith St Ninian's. In 1940 these two congregations were joined together as Leith St Ninian's Coburg Street.

Yet another strand in the history of St Ninian's Ferry Road was the Free Church congregation of North Leith. At the 1843 Disruption over 600 members left North Leith Parish Church along with most of the elders, and formed a congregation of the Free Church. At first, and for some months they worshipped in the Mariners' Kirk, which was also a Free Kirk, but in 1844 they moved into their own newly built church at the corner of Coburg Street and North Junction Street. This unpretentious building made a name for itself locally right from the start, for over the doorway there appeared a deeply incised carving of the Burning Bush—the emblem of the Scottish Church—and the date 1843. From then on 'The Burning Bush' to Leithers meant North Leith Free Kirk. The first minister, William McKenzie, was inducted in October 1844, and soon showed himself, like so many ministers of the period, an energetic evangelist and social worker. His proposal to build a Church for the Poor has already been described, and his fervent evangelism and social concern did much to strengthen and upbuild the Free Church in North Leith. His successor, Robert Macdonald, was inducted as colleague and successor to Mr McKenzie in 1857.

He came to Leith with an established reputation in the Free Church. At the first Assembly of that church in Glasgow in 1843 Mr Macdonald presented a scheme to raise £50,000 to build 500 schools. Every member of the Church would subscribe 3d to 1/- every year for five years, and no building would start until all the money had been promised. The Assembly took up the scheme with enthusiasm, and Mr Macdonald travelled all over the country explaining it and collecting subscriptions. One of the first things he noted in Leith was that his church was too small. Robert Macdonald saw that as a challenge rather than a problem. He consulted his office-bearers and agreed to raise £4000 for this work. Incredibly that sum was subscribed or promised within a few weeks, and the foundation stone of the new church in Ferry Road was laid by the Earl of Kintore in July 1858, just sixteen months after Mr Macdonald's induction. The church was opened in October 1859. A schoolroom was also added, and the total bill was £6934, more than two-thirds of which had already been paid. These are astonishing figures for a time when a respectable tradesman—a master of his trade at that—was earning about £100 a year.

The famous 'Burning Bush' of course was removed from the old building and mounted on the wall of the new church. North Leith Free Church became in 1900 North Leith United Free, and in 1929 St Nicholas Church—a name taken from the old St Nicholas Chapel which disappeared from the district when the Citadel was built in the 1650s during the Cromwellian occupation.

To return to 1982—the union under Mr Neill proved to be happy and harmonious. The minister was young, energetic and forward-looking, and the office-bearers welcomed his leadership. But there were problems. The old St Ninian's church and halls were accommodated under one roof. The halls alone were too small for the needs of the parish kirk, and North Leith desperately needed hall accommodation. Again, it was not practicable to separate St Ninian's church and halls, so that the church might be sold. The complex of buildings would only attract a buyer if it was offered as one lot. In the meantime the Boys' Brigade Halls in Ferry Road were being used, but yet more problems arose in this connection. The Brigade Halls were not church property, and were only available when not required for Brigade purposes. Ferry Road, also, was carrying more and more heavy traffic year by year, and presented a considerable risk for children crossing.

It was realized that there was only one way to overcome all these difficulties, and that was to build new hall accommodation for the parish kirk. The ground immediately north of the church, rejected a century before, when the Great Wellington Street Halls were built, was still available, and here it was decided to erect the new hall. A possible estimate of £150,000 was suggested for the project, and the first step in raising this money was the sale of the old St Ninian's buildings. Work on the new hall was put in hand and went forward steadily. Then in September 1986 Mr Neill announced that he had received a call to St Andrew's Church in Ayr, and would be transferred there in November. Members must have reflected this was reminiscent of Mr Douglas's removal to Dundee following the reconstruction of the church after the Second World War. The difficulties encountered over property, finance and the building of the new hall had now been surmounted; nothing looked likely to prevent the completion of the new building, and the call to Ayr seemed like an invitation to pastures new.

The vacancy was not prolonged. Six months after Mr Neill's departure the Rev Alistair G C McGregor, QC, BD preached as sole nominee for the charge, and was ordained and inducted on 5 August 1987. He very soon established a warm and relaxed relationship with the congregation, and had the satisfaction of seeing the completion of the new hall with the 'Burning Bush' stone mounted on the front wall.

The building was formally opened on 11 December 1987 by Mr James C McCulloch, a son of the Rev J H McCulloch, minister of North Leith from 1884 to 1912. Mr McCulloch's presence on this occasion was a remarkable link with the congregation at the turn of this century, and his reminiscences of the Edwardian congregation have been a valuable source of information in the compilation of this history. From the day of its opening the new hall has proved to be of immense benefit to the congregation, housing all kinds of activities every day of the week.

The union of North Leith and Bonnington with St Ninian's Ferry Road in 1982 marked the completion of a very long ecclesiastical pilgrimage. The original parish of North Leith, first extended to take in Newhaven in 1630, and then through succeeding centuries diversified and divided to include churches of various denominations into which the national church was fragmented, was now at last unified again within the original bounds of the parish. The congregation was born with the erection of the Chapel of St Ninian in 1493.

When that chapel became ruined it was bought and rebuilt by the people worshipping there, and so became, materially as well as spiritually, 'the people's kirk'. Before the end of the sixteenth century the congregation acquired a parish, legally established in 1606, and here an unbroken witness to the Christian faith was maintained through all vicissitudes affecting the life of both church and community. Now after five centuries the church has been restored to its status as the one national church within the bounds of the original parish. And here, in the vastly changed world of the late twentieth century, we look forward with hope and confidence to bearing the same steadfast witness to Christ in the twenty-first century that has been proclaimed by the People's Kirk in this parish through twenty generations.

APPENDIX I

Ministers of North Leith Parish

James Murehead	1599 – 1612
David Forrester	1613 – 1619, and a second term, 1627 – 1633
Henry Charteris	1620 – 1627
Andrew Fairfoul	1636 – 1652
John Knox	1653 – 1662
James Reid	1663 – 1671
Thomas Wilkie	1672 – 1687
James Hutchinson	(colleague with Thomas Wilkie) 1682 – 1687
James Lundie	1687 – 1697
Andrew Bowie	1697 – 1708
John Wilson	1708 – 1724
George Lindsay	1725 – 1764
David Johnston	1765 – 1824
Walter Foggo Ireland	Assistant and Successor to David Johnston, 1799 – 1824. Minister in sole charge, 1824 – 1828
James Buchanan	1828 – 1840
Alexander Davidson	1843 – 1858
William Smith	1860 – 1877
Robert Stewart	1877 – 1881
Andrew Wallace Williamson	1882 – 1883
John Hutton McCulloch	1884 – 1912
James Robertson Sweet Wilson	1913 – 1942
Hugh Osborne Douglas	1942 – 1951
John Heron Gibson	1952 – 1959

Andrew Stewart Todd	1960 – 1967
Douglas Clarke	1968 – 1980
William George Neill	1980 – 1986
Alistair Gerald Crichton McGregor	1987 –

APPENDIX II

List of ordained elders of North Leith Parish Church

Ordained			
1940	Mr George A M Lawrie	1981	Mr Robert Alexander
1944*	Mr John Simpson	"	Mrs Margaret Edmondston
1951	Mr D Stanley Gordon	"	Mrs Agnes Gordon
" *	Mr W McAlister	"	Mrs Rachel Inglis
1955*	Mr Kenneth McDonald	" *	Miss Muriel Linton
1956	Mr George Davidson	"	Mrs Elizabeth Mackenzie
1959	Mr Alex Arthur	"	Mrs Sarah Miller
"	Mr James Edmondston	"	Mrs Isabella Tough
" *	Mr Thomas P Lauder	1984	Mrs Marilyn Campbell
1961*	Mr Edward H Brooks	"	Mrs Eileen Doig
"	Mr Gregor Cowan	"	Mr Kenneth McAlpine
"	Mr Jack Ramsay	"	Mrs Agnes Macauley
"	Mr Sidney McLeod	1988	Mr Albert Payne
"	Mr John Melrose	"	Mr James Gibson
"	Mr George Sim	"	Mrs Catherine Sullivan
1963	Mr William Rawlings	"	Mr Robert Doig
1965*	Mr Murdoch Mackenzie	"	Miss Irene Marshall
1968	Mr William Bolt	"	Mr James Napier
"	Mr George Evans	"	Miss Ina Raeburn
1971	Mr Donald Cook	"	Miss Margaret Robertson
"	Mr Angus Gilchrist	"	Mrs Ann Whitson
1975*	Miss Jean Allan	"	Mrs Irene Wilson
"	Mrs Helen Blackwood	1989	Alex Porter
"	Mrs Janet Duncan	"	Jim Hudson
"	Mrs Jean Laidlaw	1989	Linda Dunbar
" *	Mrs Davina Mitchell	"	Bertha Hayworth
1976	Mr Andrew Campbell	"	Margaret McGregor
		"	Margaret Souza

1989	Alistair Skene	1992	Norman Lindsay
1990	Anne Lamont	"	Janette Logan
1991	Niall Martin	"	Juana Molina
1992	David Black	"	Gerry O'Neill

* non-active list